To:

_____

From:

_____

ZondervanPublishingHouse
Grand Rapids, Michigan 49530
http://www.zondervan.com

Editor: Molly Detweiler
Design: Chris Gannon
Printed in China
99 00 01 /HK/ 4 3 2 1

Previously published as *Our Daily Bread*

God's Daily Bread

BIBLE READINGS
FOR
EVERY DAY

Adapted from
Daily Light on the Daily Path Daybreak

Zondervan Gifts
We have a gift for inspiration™

January 1

THE LORD HIMSELF GOES before you and will be with you; he will never leave you nor forsake you.—Neither death nor life, neither angels nor demons, neither the present nor the future, nor any powers, neither height nor depth, nor anything else in all creation, will be able to separate us from the love of God that is in Christ Jesus our Lord.

DEUTERONOMY 31:8; ROMANS 8:38–39

January 2

THE HOUR HAS COME for you to wake up from your slumber, because our salvation is nearer now than when we first believed. The night is nearly over; the day is almost here. So let us put aside the deeds of darkness and put on the armor of light.

ROMANS 13:11–12

January 3

*I*N A DESERT LAND he found him [Jacob], in a barren and howling waste. He shielded him and cared for him; he guarded him as the apple of his eye, like an eagle that stirs up its nest and hovers over its young, that spreads its wings to catch them and carries them on its pinions.

DEUTERONOMY 32:10–11

January 4

*I*N MY FATHER'S HOUSE are many rooms; if it were not so, I would have told you. I am going there to prepare a place for you. And if I go and prepare a place for you, I will come back and take you to be with me that you also may be where I am.

JOHN 14:2–3

January 5

"COME TO ME, all you who are weary and burdened, and I will give you rest."—Therefore, since we have been justified through faith, we have peace with God through our Lord Jesus Christ, through whom we have gained access by faith into this grace in which we now stand. And we rejoice in the hope of the glory of God.

MATTHEW 11:28; ROMANS 5:1–2

January 6

MAY THE FAVOR OF the Lord our God rest upon us; establish the work of our hands for us—Blessed are all who fear the Lord, who walk in his ways. You will eat the fruit of your labor; blessings and prosperity will be yours.—Commit to the Lord whatever you do, and your plans will succeed.

PSALM 90:17; 128:1–2; PROVERBS 16:3

January 7

*I*F IT WERE I, I would appeal to God—He performs wonders that cannot be fathomed, miracles that cannot be counted."—Many, O Lord my God, are the wonders you have done. The things you planned for us no one can recount to you; were I to speak and tell of them, they would be too many to declare.

JOB 5:8–9; PSALM 40:5

January 8

*W*HO IS A GOD like you, who pardons sin and forgives the transgression of the remnant of his inheritance? You do not stay angry forever but delight to show mercy. You will again have compassion on us; you will tread our sins underfoot and hurl all our iniquities into the depths of the sea.

MICAH 7:18–19

January 9

$\mathcal{A}$S THE DEER PANTS for streams of water, so my soul pants for you, O God. My soul thirsts for God, for the living God—One thing I ask of the LORD, this is what I seek: that I may dwell in the house of the LORD all the days of my life, to gaze upon the beauty of the LORD.

PSALM 42:1–2; 27:4

January 10

"$\mathcal{B}$UT WILL GOD REALLY dwell on earth with men?"—As God has said: "I will live with them and walk among them, and I will be their God, and they will be my people."—And in him you too are being built together to become a dwelling in which God lives by his Spirit.

2 CHRONICLES 6:18; 2 CORINTHIANS 6:16;
EPHESIANS 2:22

January 11

BEFORE ME WAS A great multitude that no one could count, from every nation, tribe, people and language, standing before the throne. ...They cried out in a loud voice: "Salvation belongs to our God, who sits on the throne, and to the Lamb. ... Praise and glory and wisdom and thanks and honor and power and strength be to our God for ever and ever. Amen!"

REVELATION 7:9–10, 12

January 12

"WHEN I LIE DOWN I THINK, 'How long before I get up?'"—"Watchman, what is left of the night?" The watchman replies, "Morning is coming."—For in just a very little while, "He who is coming will come and will not delay."—He is like the light of morning at sunrise on a cloudless morning.

JOB 7:4; ISAIAH 21:11–12; HEBREWS 10:37;

2 SAMUEL 23:4

January 13

DO NOT LET THE sun go down while you are still angry.—As God's chosen people, holy and dearly loved, clothe yourselves with compassion, kindness, humility, gentleness and patience. Bear with each other and forgive whatever grievances you may have against one another. Forgive as the Lord forgave you.

EPHESIANS 4:26; COLOSSIANS 3:12–13

January 14

HIS APPEARANCE WAS SO disfigured beyond that of any man and his form marred beyond human likeness. ... But he was pierced for our transgressions, he was crushed for our iniquities; the punishment that brought us peace was upon him, and by his wounds we are healed.

ISAIAH 52:14; 53:5

January 15

SET YOUR MINDS ON things above, not on earthly things.—Our citizenship is in heaven. And we eagerly await a Savior from there, the Lord Jesus Christ, who, by the power that enables him to bring everything under his control, will transform our lowly bodies so that they will be like his glorious body.

COLOSSIANS 3:2; PHILIPPIANS 3:20–21

January 16

GOD EXALTED HIM TO the highest place and gave him the name that is above every name, that at the name of Jesus every knee should bow, in heaven and on earth and under the earth, and every tongue confess that Jesus Christ is Lord, to the glory of God the Father.

PHILIPPIANS 2:9–11

January 17

WE HAVE THE WORD of the prophets made more certain, and you will do well to pay attention to it, as to a light shining in a dark place, until the day dawns and the morning star rises in your hearts.—Your word is a lamp to my feet and a light for my path.

2 PETER 1:19; PSALM 119:105

January 18

THE LORD HIMSELF WILL come down from heaven, with a loud command, with the voice of the archangel and with the trumpet call of God, and the dead in Christ will rise first. After that, we who are still alive and are left will be caught up together with them in the clouds. ... And so we will be with the Lord forever.

1 THESSALONIANS 4:16–17

January 19

[WE] ARE JUSTIFIED FREELY by his grace through the redemption that came by Christ Jesus.—For the transgression of my people he was stricken.

ISAIAH 53:6; ROMANS 3:24; ISAIAH 53:8

January 20

HE WILL BE CALLED Wonderful Counselor.—The Word became flesh and made his dwelling among us. We have seen his glory, the glory of the One and Only who came from the Father, full of grace and truth.—"They will call him Immanuel"—which means, "God with us."

ISAIAH 9:6; JOHN 1:14; MATTHEW 1:23

January 21

BUT WE ALSO REJOICE in our sufferings, because we know that suffering produces perseverance; perseverance, character; and character, hope. And hope does not disappoint us, because God has poured out his love into our hearts by the Holy Spirit, whom he has given us.

ROMANS 5:3–5

January 22

WHEN ANXIETY WAS GREAT within me, your consolation brought joy to my soul. —I call as my heart grows faint; lead me to the rock that is higher than I.—"I am troubled; O LORD, come to my aid!"— "Take heart, son; your sins are forgiven."— "Take heart, daughter," he said, "your faith has healed you."

PSALM 94:19; 61:2; ISAIAH 38:14; MATTHEW 9:2, 22

January 23

BECAUSE GOD WANTED TO make the unchanging nature of his purpose very clear to the heirs of what was promised, he confirmed it with an oath. God did this so that ... we who have fled to take hold of the hope offered to us may be greatly encouraged. We have this hope as an anchor for the soul, firm and secure.

HEBREWS 6:17–19

January 24

"I AM THE TRUE VINE, and my Father is the gardener. He cuts off every branch in me that bears no fruit, while every branch that does bear fruit he prunes so that it will be even more fruitful. ... This is to my Father's glory, that you bear much fruit, showing yourselves to be my disciples."

JOHN 15:1–2, 8

January 25

"*I* WILL SET OUT and go back to my father
and say to him: Father, I have sinned
against heaven and against you. I am no
longer worthy to be called your son; make
me like one of your hired men.' So he got
up and went to his father."

LUKE 15:18–20

January 26

WE, WHO WITH UNVEILED faces all reflect
the Lord's glory, are being transformed into
his likeness with ever-increasing glory,
which comes from the Lord, who is the
Spirit.—What we will be has not yet been
made known. But we know that when he
appears, we shall be like him, for we shall
see him as he is.

2 CORINTHIANS 3:18; 1 JOHN 3:2

January 27

THE SON IS THE RADIANCE of God's glory and the exact representation of his being, sustaining all things by his powerful word. After he had provided purification for sins, he sat down at the right hand of the Majesty in heaven.—He was chosen before the creation of the world, but was revealed in these last times for your sake.

HEBREWS 1:3; 1 PETER 1:20

January 28

THE GOD OF ISRAEL gives power and strength to his people. Praise be to God!— He gives strength to the weary and increases the power of the weak.—I can do everything through him who gives me strength.—March on, my soul; be strong!

PSALM 68:35; ISAIAH 40:29; PHILIPPIANS 4:13;

JUDGES 5:21

January 29

I WILL PRAISE YOU, O Lord my God, with all my heart; I will glorify your name forever.... It is good to praise the Lord and make music to your name, O Most High, to proclaim your love in the morning and your faithfulness at night.... Let everything that has breath praise the Lord.

PSALM 86:12; 92:1–2; 150:6

January 30

"*I* KNOW THE PLANS I HAVE FOR YOU," declares the Lord, "plans to prosper you and not to harm you, plans to give you hope and a future."—Humble yourselves, therefore, under God's mighty hand, that he may lift you up in due time.

JEREMIAH 29:11; 1 PETER 5:6

January 31

"*I*F A MAN SINS AGAINST THE LORD, who will intercede for him?"—If anybody does sin, we have one who speaks to the Father in our defense—Christ Jesus, who died—more than that, who was raised to life—is at the right hand of God and is also interceding for us.

1 SAMUEL 2:25; 1 JOHN 2:1; ROMANS 8:34

February 1

I CONSIDER EVERYTHING A loss compared to the surpassing greatness of knowing Christ Jesus my Lord, for whose sake I have lost all things. I consider them rubbish, that I may gain Christ and be found in him, not having a righteousness of my own that comes from the law, but that which is through faith in Christ.

PHILIPPIANS 3:8–9

February 2

"*T*WO THINGS I ASK OF YOU, O LORD; do not refuse me before I die: Keep falsehood and lies far from me; give me neither poverty nor riches, but give me only my daily bread. Otherwise, I may have too much and disown you and say, 'Who is the LORD?' Or I may become poor and steal, and so dishonor the name of my God."

PROVERBS 30:7–9

February 3

*I*F YOU MAKE THE Most High your dwelling . . . then no harm will befall you, no disaster will come near your tent.—He who watches over you will not slumber. . . . The Lord is your shade at your right hand; the sun will not harm you by day, nor the moon by night. The LORD will keep you from all harm.

PSALM 91:9–10; 121:3, 5–7

February 4

*I*F THEY HAD BEEN thinking of the country they had left, they would have had opportunity to return. Instead, they were longing for a better country—a heavenly one.— "No one who puts his hand to the plow and looks back is fit for service in the kingdom of God."

HEBREWS 11:15–16; LUKE 9:62

February 5

*I*F, BY THE TRESPASS OF ONE MAN, death reigned through that one man, how much more will those who receive God's abundant provision of grace and of the gift of righteousness reign in life through the one man, Jesus Christ.—For as in Adam all die, so in Christ all will be made alive.

ROMANS 5:17; 1 CORINTHIANS 15:22

February 6

THE GRACE OF OUR Lord was poured out on me abundantly.—It is by grace you have been saved, through faith—and this not from yourselves, it is the gift of God—not by works, so that no one can boast.— Know that a man is not justified by observing the law, but by faith in Jesus Christ.

1 TIMOTHY 1:14; EPHESIANS 2:8–9; GALATIANS 2:16

February 7

JESUS CHRIST IS THE same yesterday and today and forever. . . . For we do not have a high priest who is unable to sympathize with our weaknesses, but we have one who has been tempted in every way, just as we are—yet was without sin. . . . He is able to deal gently with those who are ignorant and are going astray.

HEBREWS 13:8; 4:15; 5:2

February 8

*Y*OU ARE NO LONGER foreigners and aliens, but ... members of God's household, built on the foundation of the apostles and prophets, with Christ Jesus himself as the chief cornerstone.—As you come to him, the living Stone ... you also, like living stones, are being built into a spiritual house to be a holy priesthood, offering spiritual sacrifices acceptable to God.

EPHESIANS 2:19–20; 1 PETER 2:4–5

February 9

"*N*EVER AGAIN WILL THEY hunger; never again will they thirst. The sun will not beat upon them, nor any scorching heat. For the Lamb at the center of the throne will be their shepherd; he will lead them to springs of living water. And God will wipe away every tear from their eyes."

REVELATION 7:16–17

February 10

"*I* AM THE LIGHT of the world. Whoever follows me will never walk in darkness, but will have the light of life."—God, who said, "Let light shine out of darkness," made his light shine in our hearts to give us the light of the knowledge of the glory of God in the face of Christ.

JOHN 8:12; 2 CORINTHIANS 4:6

February 11

"*B*LESSED IS THE MAN who trusts in the LORD, whose confidence is in him. He will be like a tree planted by the water that sends out its roots by the stream. It does not fear when heat comes; its leaves are always green. It has no worries in a year of drought and never fails to bear fruit."

JEREMIAH 17:7–8

February 12

"YOU GAVE THEM TO me and they have obeyed your word.... I pray for them. I am not praying for the world, but for those you have given me, for they are yours.... And glory has come to me through them.... Father, I want those you have given me to be with me where I am, and to see my glory."

JOHN 17:6, 9–10, 24

February 13

IN HIM WAS LIFE, and that life was the light of men.... Yet to all who received him, to those who believed in his name, he gave the right to become children of God—children born not of natural descent, nor of human decision or a husband's will, but born of God.

JOHN 1:4, 12–13

February 14

"DO NOT THINK THAT I have come to abolish the Law or the Prophets; I have not come to abolish them but to fulfill them."—For what the law was powerless to do . . . God did by sending his own Son.— Christ is the end of the law so that there may be righteousness for everyone who believes.

MATTHEW 5:17; ROMANS 8:3; 10:4

February 15

MIGHTIER THAN THE THUNDER of the great waters, mightier than the breakers of the sea—the LORD on high is mighty.—O LORD God Almighty, who is like you? You are mighty, O LORD, and your faithfulness surrounds you. You rule over the surging sea; when its waves mount up, you still them.

PSALM 93:4; 89:8–9

February 16

O LORD, OUR LORD, how majestic is your name in all the earth! You have set your glory above the heavens.—And he will be called Wonderful Counselor, Mighty God, Everlasting Father, Prince of Peace.—The name of the Lord is a strong tower; the righteous run to it and are safe.

PSALM 8:1; MATTHEW 1:23; ISAIAH 9:6; PROVERBS 18:10

February 17

LET US, THEN, GO to him outside the camp, bearing the disgrace he bore.—Rejoice that you participate in the sufferings of Christ, so that you may be overjoyed when his glory is revealed.—For our light and momentary troubles are achieving for us an eternal glory that far outweighs them all.

HEBREWS 13:13; 1 PETER 4:13; 2 CORINTHIANS 4:17

February 18

[Adam] HAD A SON in his own likeness.—Surely I was sinful at birth, sinful from the time my mother conceived me.—I do not understand what I do. For what I want to do I do not do, but what I hate I do.—But thanks be to God! He gives us the victory through our Lord Jesus Christ.

Genesis 5:3; Psalm 51:5; Romans 7:15; 1 Corinthians 15:57

February 19

For the Lord gives wisdom, and from his mouth come knowledge and understanding.—If any of you lacks wisdom, he should ask God, who gives generously to all without finding fault, and it will be given to him.—It is because of him that you are in Christ Jesus, who has become for us wisdom from God.

Proverbs 2:6; James 1:5; 1 Corinthians 1:30

February 20

*E*ACH ONE IS TEMPTED when, by his own evil desire, he is dragged away and enticed. Then, after desire has conceived, it gives birth to sin.—In the desert they gave in to their craving.—"Simon, Simon, Satan has asked to sift you as wheat. But I have prayed for you, Simon, that your faith may not fail."

JAMES 1:14–15; PSALM 106:14; LUKE 22:31–32

February 21

*T*HOSE WHO SOW IN tears will reap with songs of joy. He who goes out weeping, carrying seed to sow, will return with songs of joy, carrying sheaves with him.—In this you greatly rejoice, though now for a little while you may have had to suffer grief in all kinds of trials.

PSALM 126:5–6; 1 PETER 1:6

February 22

WHETHER YOU TURN TO the right or to the left, your ears will hear a voice behind you, saying, "This is the way; walk in it."— I will instruct you and teach you in the way you should go.—I know, O LORD, that a man's life is not his own; it is not for man to direct his steps.

ISAIAH 30:21; PSALM 32:8; JEREMIAH 10:23

February 23

WHEN YOU LIE DOWN, you will not be afraid; when you lie down, your sleep will be sweet.—Do not be anxious about anything, but in everything, by prayer and petition... present your requests to God.—I will lie down and sleep in peace, for you alone, O Lord, make me dwell in safety.... He grants sleep to those he loves.

PROVERBS 3:24; PHILIPPIANS 4:6; PSALM 4:8; 127:2

February 24

YOU DO NOT HAVE, because you do not ask God.—This is the confidence we have in approaching God: that if we ask anything according to his will, he hears us.—The eyes of the LORD are on the righteous and his ears are attentive to their cry.—"Ask and you will receive, and your joy will be complete."

JAMES 4:2; 1 JOHN 5:14; PSALM 34:15; JOHN 16:24

February 25

BE STRONG IN THE Lord and in his mighty power. Put on the full armor of God so that you can take your stand against the devil's schemes.—Be self-controlled and alert. Your enemy the devil prowls around like a roaring lion looking for someone to devour. Resist him, standing firm in the faith.

EPHESIANS 6:10–11; 1 PETER 5:8–9

February 26

"*T*HIS IS THE SIGN of the covenant I am making between me and you and every living creature with you, a covenant for all generations to come: I have set my rainbow in the clouds, . . . I will see it and remember."—Has he not made with me an everlasting covenant, arranged and secured in every part?

GENESIS 9:12–13, 16; 2 SAMUEL 23:5

February 27

"*I* GIVE THEM ETERNAL life, and they shall never perish; no one can snatch them out of my hand. My Father, who has given them to me, is greater than all; no one can snatch them out of my Father's hand. I and the Father are one."—Since, then, you have been raised with Christ, set your hearts on things above.

JOHN 10:28–30; COLOSSIANS 3:1

February 28

GOD IS LOVE. This is how God showed his love among us: He sent his one and only Son into the world that we might live through him. This is love: not that we loved God, but that he loved us and sent his Son as an atoning sacrifice for our sins.... Since God so loved us, we also ought to love one another.

1 JOHN 4:8–11

February 29

"YOU ARE GOING TO have the light just a little while longer. Walk while you have the light, before darkness overtakes you. The man who walks in the dark does not know where he is going. Put your trust in the light while you have it, so that you may become sons of light."

JOHN 12:35–36

March 1

*I*F GOD IS FOR US, who can be against us?—The Lord is my light and my salvation—whom shall I fear? The Lord is the stronghold of my life—of whom shall I be afraid? —The Lord Almighty is with us; the God of Jacob is our fortress.—They will make war against the Lamb, but the Lamb will overcome them.

ROMANS 8:31; PSALM 27:1; 46:7; REVELATION 17:14

March 2

*P*RAISE BE TO . . . the Father of compassion and the God of all comfort, who comforts us in all our troubles, so that we can comfort those in any trouble with the comfort we ourselves have received from God. For just as the sufferings of Christ flow over into our lives, so also through Christ our comfort overflows.

2 CORINTHIANS 1:3–5

March 3

"*M*Y PRESENCE WILL GO WITH YOU." ...
Then Moses said to him, "If your Presence
does not go with us, do not send us up
from here. How will anyone know that
you are pleased with me and with your
people unless you go with us? What else
will distinguish me and your people from
all the other people on the face of the
earth?"

EXODUS 33:14–16

March 4

"*D*O NOT STORE UP for yourselves
treasures on earth, where moth and rust
destroy, and where thieves break in and
steal. But store up for yourselves treasures
in heaven, where moth and rust do not
destroy, and where thieves do not break in
and steal. For where your treasure is, there
your heart will be also."

MATTHEW 6:19–21

March 5

LEAD ME TO THE rock that is higher than I.
For you have been my refuge, a strong tower
against the foe. I long to dwell in your tent
forever and take refuge in the shelter of
your wings.——You have been a refuge for
the poor, a refuge for the needy in his distress, a shelter from the storm.

PSALM 61:2–4; ISAIAH 25:4

March 6

THE LORD YOUR GOD ... went ahead of
you on your journey, in fire by night and in
a cloud by day.——A righteous man may
have many troubles, but the LORD delivers
him from them all.... For the LORD watches over the way of the righteous.——"The
LORD your God is with you; he is mighty
to save."

DEUTERONOMY 1:32–33; PSALM 34:19; 1:6;

ZEPHANIAH 3:17

March 7

*T*HE WORD OF THE Lord came to Elijah: "Leave here, turn eastward and hide in the Kerith Ravine.... You will drink from the brook, and I have ordered the ravens to feed you there."—"Do not worry about your life, what you will eat or drink; or about your body, what you will wear.... your heavenly Father knows that you need them."

1 KINGS 17:2–4; MATTHEW 6:25, 32

March 8

I KNOW WHOM I HAVE BELIEVED, and am convinced that he is able.—Able to do immeasurably more than all we ask or imagine.—Able to help those who are being tempted.... Able to save completely those who come to God through him.—"Do you believe that I am able to do this?"

2 TIMOTHY 1:12; EPHESIANS 3:20; HEBREWS 2:18; 7:25;

MATTHEW 9:28

March 9

BE CAREFUL THAT YOU do not forget the Lord your God, failing to observe his commands.... Otherwise, when you eat and are satisfied, when you build fine houses and settle down,... then your heart will become proud and you will forget the Lord your God.... But remember the Lord your God, for it is he who gives you the ability to produce wealth.

DEUTERONOMY 8:11–12; 14, 18

March 10

"WHERE TWO OR THREE come together in my name, there am I with them."—"If anyone loves me, he will obey my teaching. My Father will love him, and we will come to him and make our home with him."— "If you obey my commands, you will remain in my love, just as I have obeyed my Father's commands and remain in his love."

MATTHEW 18:20; JOHN 14:23; 15:10

March 11

"*H*OLY FATHER, PROTECT THEM by the power of your name—the name you gave me—so that they may be one as we are one. While I was with them, I protected them and kept them safe by that name you gave me."—The Lord will rescue me from every evil attack and will bring me safely to his heavenly kingdom.

JOHN 17:11–12; 2 TIMOTHY 4:18

March 12

*D*O WHAT PLEASES HIM.—For the Lord takes delight in his people. —I will praise God's name in song and glorify him with thanksgiving. This will please the Lord.— Therefore, I urge you, brothers, in view of God's mercy, to offer your bodies as living sacrifices, holy and pleasing to God.

1 JOHN 3:22; PSALM 149:4; 69:30–31; ROMANS 12:1

March 13

*F*OR THERE IS ONE God and one mediator between God and men, the man Christ Jesus.—We have one who speaks to the Father in our defense—Jesus Christ, the Righteous One.—He entered the Most Holy Place once for all by his own blood, having obtained eternal redemption. . . . For this reason Christ is the mediator of a new covenant.

1 TIMOTHY 2:5; 1 JOHN 2:1; HEBREWS 9:12, 15

March 14

*H*OW CAN A YOUNG man keep his way pure? By living according to your word. . . . I have hidden your word in my heart that I might not sin against you. . . . The law from your mouth is more precious to me than thousands of pieces of silver and gold. . . . I will never forget your precepts, for by them you have renewed my life.

PSALM 119:9, 11, 72, 93

March 15

*T*HE LORD MADE THE heavens and the
earth, the sea, and all that is in them.—
The heavens declare the glory of God; the
skies proclaim the work of his hands. —By
the word of the Lord were the heavens
made, their starry host by the breath of his
mouth.... He spoke, and it came to be; he
commanded, and it stood firm.

EXODUS 20:11; PSALM 19:1; 33:6, 9

March 16

*M*Y MOUTH WILL SPEAK in praise of the
LORD. Let every creature praise his holy
name for ever and ever.—Praise the Lord.
How good it is to sing praises to our God,
how pleasant and fitting to praise him!...
Sing to the LORD with thanksgiving; make
music to our God on the harp.

PSALM 145:21; 147:1, 7

March 17

THE DEVIL . . . SHOWED HIM all the kingdoms of the world and their splendor. "All
this I will give you," he said, "if you will
bow down and worship me." Jesus said to
him, "Away from me, Satan!"—Because he
himself suffered when he was tempted,
he is able to help those who are being
tempted.

MATTHEW 4:8–10; HEBREWS 2:18

March 18

THEY WERE LOOKING INTENTLY up into
the sky as he was going, when suddenly two
men dressed in white stood beside them.
"Men of Galilee," they said, "why do you
stand here looking into the sky? This same
Jesus, who has been taken from you into
heaven, will come back in the same way you
have seen him go into heaven."

ACTS 1:10–11

March 19

"*H*EAVEN AND EARTH WILL pass away,
but my words will never pass away."—"You
know with all your heart and soul that not
one of all the good promises the LORD
your God gave you has failed. Every
promise has been fulfilled; not one has
failed."

LUKE 21:33; JOSHUA 23:14

March 20

*G*OD IS LIGHT; in him there is no darkness
at all.—You were once darkness, but now
you are light in the Lord. Live as children
of light.—You are a chosen people, a royal
priesthood, a holy nation, a people belonging to God, . . . who called you out of darkness into his wonderful light.

1 JOHN 1:5; EPHESIANS 5:8; 1 PETER 2:9

March 21

THE END OF ALL THINGS IS NEAR. Therefore be clear minded and self-controlled so that you can pray.—Only be careful, and watch yourselves closely so that you do not forget the things your eyes have seen or let them slip from your heart as long as you live.—"What I say to you, I say to everyone: 'Watch!'"

1 PETER 4:7; DEUTERONOMY 4:9; MARK 13:37

March 22

GOD HAS SAID, "Never will I leave you; never will I forsake you."—Stand firm then, with the belt of truth buckled around your waist, with the breastplate of righteousness in place.... Put on the full armor of God, so that when the day of evil comes, you may be able to stand your ground, and after you have done everything, to stand.

HEBREWS 13:5; EPHESIANS 6:14, 13

March 23

"*H*OLY, HOLY, HOLY IS the Lord God Almighty."—"I am the God of your father, the God of Abraham, the God of Isaac and the God of Jacob."—"To whom will you compare me? Or who is my equal?" ... "I am the Lord, your God, the Holy One of Israel, your Savior."—"Be holy, because I am holy."

REVELATION 4:8; EXODUS 3:6; ISAIAH 40:25, 43:3;
1 PETER 1:16

March 24

*A*BRAM BELIEVED THE LORD.—He did not waver through unbelief regarding the promise of God, but was strengthened in his faith and gave glory to God, being fully persuaded that God had power to do what he had promised.—Let us hold unswervingly to the hope we profess, for he who promised is faithful.

GENESIS 15:6; ROMANS 4:20–21; HEBREWS 10:23

March 25

"MASTER, WE'VE WORKED HARD all night and haven't caught anything. But because you say so, I will let down the nets."— "The kingdom of heaven is like a net that was let down into the lake."—Let us not become weary in doing good, for at the proper time we will reap a harvest if we do not give up.

LUKE 5:5; MATTHEW 13:47; GALATIANS 6:9

March 26

SHARE WITH GOD'S PEOPLE who are in need.—"I was hungry and you gave me something to eat, I was thirsty and you gave me something to drink, I was a stranger and you invited me in, I needed clothes and you clothed me."—Do not forget to do good and to share with others, for with such sacrifices God is pleased.

ROMANS 12:13; MATTHEW 25:35–36; HEBREWS 13:16

March 27

"THE MAN WHO HAD received the five talents brought the other five. 'Master,' he said, 'you entrusted me with five talents. See, I have gained five more.' His master replied, 'Well done, good and faithful servant! You have been faithful with a few things; I will put you in charge of many things. Come and share your master's happiness!'"

MATTHEW 25:20–21

March 28

HE GIVES STRENGTH TO the weary and increases the power of the weak. Even youths grow tired and weary, and young men stumble and fall; but those who hope in the Lord will renew their strength. They will soar on wings like eagles; they will run and not grow weary, they will walk and not be faint.

ISAIAH 40:29–31

March 29

"DO NOT BE AFRAID, little flock, for your Father has been pleased to give you the kingdom."—Has not God chosen those who are poor in the eyes of the world to be rich in faith and to inherit the kingdom he promised those who love him?—Now if we are children, then we are heirs—heirs of God and co-heirs with Christ.

LUKE 12:32; JAMES 2:5; ROMANS 8:17

March 30

BLESSED IS THE MAN who does not walk in the counsel of the wicked or stand in the way of sinners or sit in the seat of mockers. But his delight is in the law of the LORD, and on his law he meditates day and night.—"Do not let this Book of the Law depart from your mouth; meditate on it day and night."

PSALM 1:1–2; JOSHUA 1:8

March 31

THE WAY OF THE wicked is like deep darkness; they do not know what makes them stumble. —The path of the righteous is like the first gleam of dawn, shining ever brighter till the full light of day.—
"I have come into the world as a light, so that no one who believes in me should stay in darkness."

PROVERBS 4:19, 18; JOHN 12:46

April 1

"YOU WILL HAVE A son who will be a man of peace and rest.... His name will be Solomon, and I will grant Israel peace and quiet during his reign."—"One greater than Solomon is here."—He will be called... Prince of Peace.—For he himself is our peace.

1 CHRONICLES 22:9; MATTHEW 12:42; ISAIAH 9:6;

EPHESIANS 2:14

April 2

DEAR CHILDREN, KEEP YOURSELVES from idols.—"Do not worship any other god, for the LORD, whose name is Jealous, is a jealous God."—"Serve him with whole-hearted devotion and with a willing mind, for the LORD searches every heart and understands every motive behind the thoughts."

1 JOHN 5:21; EXODUS 34:14; 1 CHRONICLES 28:9

April 3

WITH THE LORD A day is like a thousand years, and a thousand years are like a day.— "For my thoughts are not your thoughts, neither are your ways my ways," declares the Lord. "As the heavens are higher than the earth, so are my ways higher than your ways and my thoughts than your thoughts."

2 PETER 3:8; ISAIAH 55:8–9

April 4

"YOU WERE LIKE A burning stick snatched from the fire."—Since, then, we know what it is to fear the LORD, we try to persuade men.—Snatch others from the fire and save them.—"By my Spirit," says the LORD.— Who wants all men to be saved and to come to a knowledge of the truth.

AMOS 4:11; 2 CORINTHIANS 5:11; JUDE 23;
ZECHARIAH 4:6; 1 TIMOTHY 2:4

April 5

JESUS ANSWERED, "Woman, you have great faith! Your request is granted." ... "According to your faith will it be done to you."—But when he asks, he must believe and not doubt, because he who doubts is like a wave of the sea, blown and tossed by the wind. That man should not think he will receive anything from the Lord.

MATTHEW 15:28; 9:29; JAMES 1:6—7

April 6

CHRIST DID NOT ENTER a man-made sanctuary that was only a copy of the true one; he entered heaven itself, now to appear for us in God's presence.... Let us then approach the throne of grace with confidence, so that we may receive mercy and find grace to help us in our time of need.

HEBREWS 9:24; 4:16

April 7

"MY GRACE IS SUFFICIENT for you, for my power is made perfect in weakness." Therefore I will boast all the more gladly about my weaknesses, so that Christ's power may rest on me.—I can do everything through him who gives me strength.

2 CORINTHIANS 12:9; PHILIPPIANS 4:13

April 8

"REMAIN IN ME, AND I will remain in you. No branch can bear fruit by itself; it must remain in the vine.... I am the vine; you are the branches. If a man remains in me and I in him, he will bear much fruit." ... "If you remain in me and my words remain in you, ask whatever you wish, and it will be given you."

JOHN 15:4–5; 7

April 9

I WILL TELL OF the kindnesses of the Lord, the deeds for which he is to be praised.—He lifted me out of the slimy pit, out of the mud and mire; he set my feet on a rock and gave me a firm place to stand.—God raised us up with Christ and seated us with him in the heavenly realms.

ISAIAH 63:7; PSALM 40:2; EPHESIANS 2:6

April 10

SURELY I WAS SINFUL at birth, sinful from the time my mother conceived me.— "... Lord; I am a sinful man!"— "Therefore, I despise myself and repent in dust and ashes."—When I want to do good, evil is right there with me.—"Take heart, son; your sins are forgiven."

PSALM 51:5; LUKE 5:8; JOB 42:6; ROMANS 7:21; MATTHEW 9:2

April 11

EVERYONE SHOULD BE QUICK to listen, slow to speak and slow to become angry.— Better a patient man than a warrior, a man who controls his temper than one who takes a city.—When they hurled their insults at him, he did not retaliate; when he suffered, he made no threats. Instead, he entrusted himself to him who judges justly.

JAMES 1:19; PROVERBS 16:32; 1 PETER 2:23

April 12

THE LAW IS ONLY a shadow of the good
things that are coming—not the realities
themselves. For this reason it can never, by
the same sacrifices repeated endlessly year
after year, make perfect those who draw
near to worship. If it could, would they not
have stopped being offered?—Through
him everyone who believes is justified.

HEBREWS 10:1–2; ACTS 13:39

April 13

THERE WILL BE NO night there.—For the
LORD will be your everlasting light, and
your God will be your glory.—The city
does not need the sun or the moon to shine
on it, for the glory of God gives it light,
and the Lamb is its lamp.

REVELATION 21:25; ISAIAH 60:19; REVELATION 21:23

April 14

*H*OW PRECIOUS TO ME are your thoughts, O God! How vast is the sum of them! Were I to count them, they would outnumber the grains of sand. —How sweet are your words to my taste, sweeter than honey to my mouth!—Your love is more delightful than wine.—And earth has nothing I desire besides you.

PSALM 139:17–18; 119:103; SONG OF SONGS 1:2;

PSALM 73:25

April 15

*W*HO SHALL SEPARATE US from the love of Christ?... For I am convinced that neither death nor life, neither angels nor demons, neither the present nor the future, nor any powers, neither height nor depth, nor anything else in all creation, will be able to separate us from the love of God that is in Christ Jesus our Lord.

ROMANS 8:35, 38–39

April 16

*T*HAT NIGHT GOD APPEARED to Solomon and said to him, "Ask for whatever you want me to give you." Solomon answered God, ... "Give me wisdom and knowledge, that I may lead this people."—God gave Solomon wisdom and very great insight, and a breadth of understanding as measureless as the sand on the seashore.

2 CHRONICLES 1:7–8, 10; 1 KINGS 4:29

April 17

*Y*OU ARE A CHOSEN people, a royal priesthood, a holy nation, a people belonging to God, that you may declare the praises of him who called you out of darkness into his wonderful light.—My soul will boast in the LORD; let the afflicted hear and rejoice. Glorify the LORD with me; let us exalt his name together.

1 PETER 2:9; PSALM 34:2–3

April 18

"*T*AKE MY YOKE UPON you and learn from me, for I am gentle and humble in heart, and you will find rest for your souls."— Your attitude should be the same as that of Christ Jesus: Who, being in very nature God, did not consider equality with God something to be grasped, but made himself nothing, taking the very nature of a servant.

MATTHEW 11:29; PHILIPPIANS 2:5–7

April 19

*H*IS WORD IS IN my heart like a fire, a fire shut up in my bones. I am weary of holding it in; indeed, I cannot.—"We cannot help speaking about what we have seen and heard."—For Christ's love compels us.— "Go home to your family and tell them how much the Lord has done for you."

JEREMIAH 20:9; ACTS 4:20; 2 CORINTHIANS 5:14; MARK 5:19

April 20

"WHEN YOU PASS THROUGH the waters, I
will be with you; and when you pass
through the rivers, they will not sweep over
you. When you walk through the fire, you
will not be burned; the flames will not set
you ablaze. For I am the LORD, your God,
the Holy One of Israel, your Savior."

ISAIAH 43:2–3

April 21

MY FEET HAVE CLOSELY followed his
steps; I have kept to his way without turn-
ing aside.—"If you hold to my teaching,
you are really my disciples."—"He who
stands firm to the end will be saved."—
"He who overcomes will ... be dressed in
white. I will never blot out his name from
the book of life."

JOB 23:11; JOHN 8:31; MATTHEW 24:13; REVELATION 3:5

April 22

"GOD HIMSELF WILL PROVIDE the lamb for the burnt offering, my son."—"Look, the Lamb of God, who takes away the sin of the world!"—"A ransom for many."— God made him who had no sin to be sin for us, so that in him we might become the righteousness of God.

GENESIS 22:8; JOHN 1:29; MATTHEW 20:28;

2 CORINTHIANS 5:21

April 23

"MY SHEEP LISTEN TO my voice; I know them, and they follow me."—"Suppose one of you has a hundred sheep and loses one of them. Does he not leave the ninety-nine in the open country and go after the lost sheep until he finds it?"

JOHN 10:27; LUKE 15:4

April 24

THE LORD WAS GRACIOUS to Sarah as he had said, and the LORD did for Sarah what he had promised.—Trust in him at all times, O people.—Does he speak and then not act? Does he promise and not fulfill?— "The grass withers and the flowers fall, but the word of our God stands forever."

GENESIS 21:1; PSALM 62:8; NUMBERS 23:19; ISAIAH 40:8

April 25

THE SON IS THE radiance of God's glory and the exact representation of his being, sustaining all things by his powerful word. After he had provided purification for sins, he sat down at the right hand of the Majesty in heaven. So he became as much superior to the angels as the name he has inherited is superior to theirs.

HEBREWS 1:3–4

April 26

WHEN HE SAW THE WIND, he was afraid and, beginning to sink, cried out, "Lord, save me!" Immediately Jesus reached out his hand and caught him.—If the LORD delights in a man's way, he makes his steps firm; though he stumble, he will not fall, for the LORD upholds him with his hand.

MATTHEW 14:30–31; PSALM 37:23–24

April 27

THE WORLD AND ITS desires pass away, but the man who does the will of God lives forever.—You need to persevere so that when you have done the will of God, you will receive what he has promised. For in just a very little while, "He who is coming will come and will not delay."

1 JOHN 2:17; HEBREWS 10:36–37

April 28

"*I*T WAS NOT WITH perishable things such
as silver or gold that you were redeemed
from the empty way of life handed
down to you from your forefathers, but
with the precious blood of Christ, a lamb
without blemish or defect."—"Worthy
is the Lamb, who was slain, to receive power
and wealth and wisdom and strength and
honor and glory and praise!"

1 PETER 1:18–19; REVELATION 5:12

April 29

I KNOW, O Lord, that your laws are righteous, and in faithfulness you have afflicted
me.—Before I was afflicted I went astray,
but now I obey your word.—The Lord has
chastened me severely, but he has not given
me over to death.—He does not treat us as
our sins deserve or repay us according to
our iniquities.

PSALM 119:75, 67; 118:18; 103:10

April 30

"THE LORD, THE LORD, the compassionate and gracious God, slow to anger,
abounding in love and faithfulness."
—The Lord is not slow in keeping his
promise, as some understand slowness. He
is patient with you, not wanting anyone to
perish, but everyone to come to
repentance.—Be imitators of God, therefore, as dearly loved children.

EXODUS 34:6; 2 PETER 3:9; EPHESIANS 5:1

May 1

THE FRUIT OF THE Spirit is ... peace...
God has called us to live in peace.—"Peace
I leave with you; my peace I give you."—
May the God of hope fill you with all joy
and peace as you trust in him.—The fruit
of righteousness will be peace.

GALATIANS 5:22; 1 CORINTHIANS 7:15; JOHN 14:27;

ROMANS 15:13; ISAIAH 32:17

May 2

*W*HERE CAN I GO from your Spirit? Where can I flee from your presence? If I go up to the heavens, you are there; if I make my bed in the depths, you are there.—"Am I only a God nearby," declares the LORD, "and not a God far away? Can anyone hide in secret places so that I cannot see him?"

PSALM 139:7–8; JEREMIAH 23:23–24

May 3

"*I* AM GOD ALMIGHTY; walk before me and be blameless."—Blessed are they whose ways are blameless, who walk according to the law of the Lord.—The man who looks intently into the perfect law that gives freedom, and continues to do this, not forgetting what he has heard, but doing it—he will be blessed in what he does.

GENESIS 17:1; PSALM 119:1; JAMES 1:25

May 4

SURELY THE ARM OF the Lord is not too short to save, nor his ear too dull to hear.—When I called, you answered me; you made me bold and stouthearted.—"Ah, Sovereign Lord, you have made the heavens and the earth by your great power and out-stretched arm. Nothing is too hard for you."

ISAIAH 59:1; PSALM 138:3; JEREMIAH 32:17

May 5

FEAR THE LORD, YOU his saints, for those who fear him lack nothing. The lions may grow weak and hungry, but those who seek the LORD lack no good thing.... No good thing does he withhold from those whose walk is blameless. O LORD Almighty, blessed is the man who trusts in you.

PSALM 34:9–10; 84:11–12

May 6

*B*Y DAY THE Lord went ahead of them in a pillar of cloud to guide them on their way and by night in a pillar of fire to give them light, so that they could travel by day or night. Neither the pillar of cloud by day nor the pillar of fire by night left its place in front of the people.

EXODUS 13:21–22

May 7

"*Y*OU WILL HEAR OF wars and rumors of wars, but see to it that you are not alarmed."—He will have no fear of bad news; his heart is steadfast, trusting in the Lord.—"I have told you these things, so that in me you may have peace. In this world you will have trouble. But take heart! I have overcome the world."

MATTHEW 24:6; PSALM 112:7; JOHN 16:33

May 8

"WHAT SHALL I SAY? 'Father, save me from this hour?' No, it was for this very reason I came."—"Not my will, but yours be done."—"The one who sent me is with me; he has not left me alone, for I always do what pleases him."—"This is my Son, whom I love; with him I am well pleased."

JOHN 12:27; LUKE 22:42; JOHN 8:29; MATTHEW 3:17

May 9

"WOE TO ME!" I cried. "I am ruined! For I am a man of unclean lips." . . . Then one of the seraphs flew to me with a live coal in his hand, which he had taken with tongs from the altar. With it he touched my mouth and said, "See, this has touched your lips; your guilt is taken away and your sin atoned for."

ISAIAH 6:5–7

May 10

*H*ERE WE DO NOT have an enduring city, but we are looking for the city that is to come.—Our citizenship is in heaven. And we eagerly await a Savior from there, the Lord Jesus Christ, who, by the power that enables him to bring everything under his control, will transform our lowly bodies so that they will be like his glorious body.

HEBREWS 13:14; PHILIPPIANS 3:20–21

May 11

*R*ID YOURSELVES OF ALL the offenses you have committed, and get a new heart and a new spirit.—Get rid of all moral filth and the evil that is so prevalent, and humbly accept the word planted in you, which can save you.—Continue in him, so that when he appears we may be confident and unashamed before him.

EZEKIEL 18:31; JAMES 1:21; 1 JOHN 2:28

May 12

SCORN HAS BROKEN MY HEART.—"Isn't this the carpenter's son?"—"Nazareth! Can anything good come from there?"—"This man is a sinner."—"He deceives the people."—"This fellow is blaspheming!"—"Here is a glutton and a drunkard."—If you are insulted because of the name of Christ, you are blessed.

PSALM 69:20; MATTHEW 13:55; JOHN 1:46; 9:24; 7:12;
MATTHEW 9:3; 11:19; 1 PETER 4:14

May 13

I WANT MEN EVERYWHERE to lift up holy hands in prayer, without anger or disputing.—"A time is coming and has now come when the true worshipers will worship the Father in spirit and truth, for they are the kind of worshipers the Father seeks. God is spirit, and his worshipers must worship in spirit and in truth."

1 TIMOTHY 2:8; JOHN 4:23–24

May 14

*H*E WAS DESPISED AND rejected by men, a man of sorrows, and familiar with suffering. Like one from whom men hide their faces he was despised.—Let us fix our eyes on Jesus, the author and perfecter of our faith, who for the joy set before him endured the cross, scorning its shame, and sat down at the right hand of the throne of God.

ISAIAH 53:3; HEBREWS 12:2

May 15

"*H*E WILL WIPE EVERY tear from their eyes. There will be no more death or mourning or crying or pain, for the old order of things has passed away."—The Sovereign LORD will wipe away the tears from all faces.... Sorrow and sighing will flee away.

REVELATION 21:4; ISAIAH 25:8; 35:10

May 16

*T*RUST IN THE Lord with all your heart and lean not on your own understanding; in all your ways acknowledge him, and he will make your paths straight.—You guide me with your counsel, and afterward you will take me into glory.—For this God is our God for ever and ever; he will be our guide even to the end.

PROVERBS 3:5–6; PSALM 73:24; 48:14

May 17

I AM THE Lord your God; follow my decrees and be careful to keep my laws.— Whoever keeps the whole law and yet stumbles at just one point is guilty of breaking all of it.—Teach me, O LORD, to follow your decrees.—It is God who works in you to will and to act according to his good purpose.

EZEKIEL 20:19; JAMES 2:10; PSALM 119:33;

PHILIPPIANS 2:13

May 18

"*H*OLY IS THE LORD God Almighty, who was, and is, and is to come." . . . who lives for ever and ever.—The blessed and only Ruler, the King of kings and Lord of lords, who alone is immortal and who lives in unapproachable light, whom no one has seen or can see.—The King eternal, immortal, invisible, the only God.

REVELATION 4:8–9; 1 TIMOTHY 6:15–16; 1:17

May 19

"*M*Y PRAYER IS NOT for them alone. I pray also for those who will believe in me through their message, that all of them may be one, Father, just as you are in me and I am in you. May they also be in us so that the world may believe that you have sent me."

JOHN 17:20–21

May 20

*E*VERYONE WHO COMPETES IN the games goes into strict training. They do it to get a crown that will not last; but we do it to get a crown that will last forever. Therefore ... I beat my body and make it my slave so that after I have preached to others, I myself will not be disqualified for the prize.

1 CORINTHIANS 9:25–27

May 21

"*Y*OU CALL ME 'TEACHER' and 'Lord,' and rightly so, for that is what I am. Now that I, your Lord and Teacher, have washed your feet, you also should wash one another's feet. I have set you an example that you should do as I have done for you."

JOHN 13:13–15

May 22

MAN IS A MERE phantom as he goes to and fro: He bustles about, but only in vain.—"Martha, Martha," the Lord answered, "you are worried and upset about many things, but only one thing is needed. Mary has chosen what is better, and it will not be taken away from her."

PSALM 39:6; LUKE 10:41–42

May 23

WHO IS LIKE THE Lord our God, the One who sits enthroned on high, who stoops down to look on the heavens and the earth?—He does as he pleases with the powers of heaven and the peoples of the earth.—The eyes of the Lord range throughout the earth to strengthen those whose hearts are fully committed to him.

PSALM 113:5–6; DANIEL 4:35; 2 CHRONICLES 16:9

May 24

"So HE GOT UP and went to his father. But while he was still a long way off, his father saw him and was filled with compassion for him; he ran to his son, threw his arms around him and kissed him."—If we confess our sins, he is faithful and just and will forgive us our sins and purify us from all unrighteousness.

LUKE 15:20; 1 JOHN 1:9

May 25

YOU HAVE MADE KNOWN to me the path of life; you will fill me with joy in your presence, with eternal pleasures at your right hand.... How priceless is your unfailing love! Both high and low among men find refuge in the shadow of your wings.... For with you is the fountain of life; in your light we see light.

PSALM 16:11; 36:7, 9

May 26

"*I* AM THE GOOD shepherd; I know my sheep." . . . "I give them eternal life." . . . "The good shepherd lays down his life for the sheep."—"I will search for the lost and bring back the strays. I will bind up the injured and strengthen the weak."

JOHN 10:14, 28, 11; EZEKIEL 34:16

May 27

*G*OD IS OUR REFUGE and strength, an ever-present help in trouble.—I will say of the LORD, "He is my refuge and my fortress, my God, in whom I trust."—"He is a shield for all who take refuge in him. For who is God besides the LORD? And who is the Rock except our God?"

PSALM 46:1; 91:2; 2 SAMUEL 22:31–32

May 28

THIS WORLD IN ITS present form is passing away.—But in keeping with his promise we are looking forward to a new heaven and a new earth, the home of righteousness. So then, dear friends, since you are looking forward to this, make every effort to be found spotless, blameless and at peace with him.

1 CORINTHIANS 7:31; 2 PETER 3:13–14

May 29

THE LIFE OF A creature is in the blood.... It is the blood that makes atonement for one's life.—Without the shedding of blood there is no forgiveness.—The blood of Jesus, his Son, purifies us from all sin.— You were bought at a price. Therefore honor God with your body.

LEVITICUS 17:11; HEBREWS 9:22; 1 JOHN 1:7;

1 CORINTHIANS 6:20

May 30

LET US, THEREFORE, MAKE every effort to enter that rest.—"Enter through the narrow gate. For wide is the gate and broad is the road that leads to destruction, and many enter through it. But small is the gate and narrow the road that leads to life, and only a few find it."

HEBREWS 4:11; MATTHEW 7:13–14

May 31

"HAVE FAITH IN GOD," Jesus answered. "I tell you the truth, if anyone says to this mountain, 'Go, throw yourself into the sea,' and does not doubt in his heart but believes that what he says will happen, it will be done for him. Therefore I tell you, whatever you ask for in prayer, believe that you have received it, and it will be yours."

MARK 11:22–24

June 1

*L*IVE A LIFE WORTHY of the calling you have received. Be completely humble and gentle; be patient, bearing with one another in love.... Be kind and compassionate to one another, forgiving each other, just as in Christ God forgave you.—Love is patient, love is kind.

EPHESIANS 4:1–2, 32; 1 CORINTHIANS 13:4

June 2

"*B*E DRESSED READY FOR service and keep your lamps burning, like men waiting for their master to return from a wedding banquet, so that when he comes and knocks they can immediately open the door for him. It will be good for those servants whose master finds them watching when he comes."

LUKE 12:35–37

June 3

"MY PRAYER IS NOT that you take them out of the world but that you protect them from the evil one.... I in them and you in me. May they be brought to complete unity to let the world know that you sent me and have loved them even as you have loved me."

JOHN 17:15, 23

June 4

RIGHTEOUSNESS FROM GOD COMES through faith in Jesus Christ to all who believe.—For he ... arrayed me in a robe of righteousness.—You were once darkness, but you are light in the Lord. Live as children of light.... Have nothing to do with the fruitless deeds of darkness, but rather expose them.

ROMANS 3:22; ISAIAH 61:10; EPHESIANS 5:8, 11

June 5

AS A FATHER HAS compassion on his children, so the Lord has compassion on those who fear him.—He was merciful; he forgave their iniquities and did not destroy them. Time after time he restrained his anger and did not stir up his full wrath. He remembered that they were but flesh, a passing breeze that does not return.

PSALM 103:13; 78:38–39

June 6

WITHOUT HOLINESS NO ONE will see the Lord.—"I am the way and the truth and the life. No one comes to the Father except through me."—He himself is our peace, who has ... destroyed the barrier, the dividing wall of hostility.—The curtain of the temple was torn in two from top to bottom.

HEBREWS 12:14; JOHN 14:6; EPHESIANS 2:14;

MATTHEW 27:51

June 7

"COME NOW, LET US REASON TOGETHER," says the LORD. "Though your sins are like scarlet, they shall be as white as snow; though they are red as crimson, they shall be like wool."—"I, even I, am he who blots out your transgressions, for my own sake, and remembers your sins no more."

ISAIAH 1:18; 43:25

June 8

"LOOK AT THE BIRDS of the air . . . your heavenly Father feeds them. Are you not much more valuable than they?"—"Why are you talking among yourselves about having no bread? . . . Don't you remember the five loaves for the five thousand?"—My God will meet all your needs according to his glorious riches in Christ Jesus.

MATTHEW 6:26; 16:8–9; PHILIPPIANS 4:19

June 9

"No one ever spoke the way this man does."—The Sovereign LORD has given me an instructed tongue, to know the word that sustains the weary.—All spoke well of him and were amazed at the gracious words that came from his lips.—He taught as one who had authority, and not as their teachers of the law.

JOHN 7:46; ISAIAH 50:4; LUKE 4:22; MATTHEW 7:29

June 10

Bear with each other and forgive whatever grievances you may have against one another. Forgive as the Lord forgave you.—"Lord, how many times shall I forgive my brother when he sins against me? Up to seven times?" Jesus answered, "I tell you, not seven times, but seventy-seven times."

COLOSSIANS 3:13; MATTHEW 18:21–22

June 11

"No one can see the kingdom of God unless he is born again."—If anyone is in Christ, he is a new creation; the old has gone, the new has come!—"I will give you a new heart and put a new spirit in you; I will remove from you your heart of stone and give you a heart of flesh."

John 3:3; 2 Corinthians 5:17; Ezekiel 36:26

June 12

The Lord your God is testing you to find out whether you love him with all your heart and with all your soul.—For you, O God, tested us; you refined us like silver. . . . we went through fire and water, but you brought us to a place of abundance.— When you walk through the fire, you will not be burned.

Deuteronomy 13:3; Psalm 66:10, 12; Isaiah 43:2

June 13

*T*HE LIFE I LIVE in the body, I live by faith in the Son of God, who loved me and gave himself for me.—Dear children, continue in him, so that when he appears we may be confident and unashamed before him at his coming. . . . Whoever claims to live in him must walk as Jesus did.

GALATIANS 2:20; 1 JOHN 2:28, 6

June 14

*I*F WE HAVE FOOD and clothing, we will be content with that. People who want to get rich fall into temptation and a trap and into many foolish and harmful desires that plunge men into ruin and destruction. For the love of money is a root of all kinds of evil. Some people, eager for money, have wandered from the faith.

1 TIMOTHY 6:8–10

June 15

*T*HE SECRET THINGS BELONG to the Lord our God, but the things revealed belong to us.——"I no longer call you servants, because a servant does not know his master's business. Instead, I have called you friends, for everything that I learned from my Father I have made known to you."

DEUTERONOMY 29:29; JOHN 15:15

June 16

*B*E VERY CAREFUL, THEN, how you live— not as unwise but as wise.——"Be very careful to keep the commandment and the law ... to love the Lord your God, to walk in all his ways, to obey his commands, to hold fast to him and to serve him with all your heart and all your soul."

EPHESIANS 5:15; JOSHUA 22:5

June 17

BECAUSE YOUR LOVE IS better than life, my lips will glorify you. I will praise you as long as I live, and in your name I will lift up my hands. My soul will be satisfied as with the richest of foods; with singing lips my mouth will praise you.

PSALM 63:3–5

June 18

LET US DRAW NEAR to God with a sincere heart in full assurance of faith, having our hearts sprinkled to cleanse us from a guilty conscience and having our bodies washed with pure water. . . . Let us then approach the throne of grace with confidence, so that we may receive mercy and find grace to help us in our time of need.

HEBREWS 10:22; 4:16

June 19

"No one who has left home or brothers or sisters or mother or father or children or fields for me and the gospel will fail to receive a hundred times as much in this present age (homes, brothers, sisters, mothers, children and fields—and with them, persecutions) and in the age to come, eternal life."

MARK 10:29–30

June 20

If you make the Most High your dwelling—even the Lord, who is my refuge—then no harm will befall you, no disaster will come near your tent. For he will command his angels concerning you to guard you in all your ways.—When you lie down, you will not be afraid; when you lie down, your sleep will be sweet.

PSALM 91:9–11; PROVERBS 3:24

June 21

CHRIST SUFFERED FOR YOU, leaving you an example, that you should follow in his steps.—"Even the Son of Man did not come to be served, but to serve."... "Whoever wants to be first must be slave of all."—Carry each other's burdens, and in this way you will fulfill the law of Christ.

1 PETER 2:21; MARK 10:45, 44; GALATIANS 6:2

June 22

SEE HOW HE LOVED HIM!... "Greater love has no one than this, that one lay down his life for his friends."... Having loved his own who were in the world, he now showed them the full extent of his love.—We love because he first loved us.

JOHN 11:36; 15:13; 13:1; 1 JOHN 4:19

June 23

"SHOULD I NOT TRY to find a home for you, where you will be well provided for?"—My people will live in peaceful dwelling places, in secure homes, in undisturbed places of rest.—The Lord is my shepherd, I shall lack nothing. He makes me lie down in green pastures, he leads me beside quiet waters.

RUTH 3:1; ISAIAH 32:18; PSALM 23:1–2

June 24

"IN MY FATHER'S HOUSE are many rooms; if it were not so, I would have told you. I am going there to prepare a place for you. And if I go and prepare a place for you, I will come back and take you to be with me that you also may be where I am."

JOHN 14:2–3

June 25

WE KNOW THAT WHEN he appears we
shall be like him, for we shall see him as he
is.—Now we see but a poor reflection;
then we shall see face to face.—In righteousness I will see your face; when I awake,
I will be satisfied with seeing your likeness.

1 JOHN 3:2; 1 CORINTHIANS 13:12; PSALM 17:15

June 26

"ASK AND IT WILL be given to you; seek
and you will find; knock and the door will
be opened to you. For everyone who asks
receives; he who seeks finds; and to him
who knocks, the door will be opened."

MATTHEW 7:7–8

June 27

WHO CAN ENDURE THE day of his coming? Who can stand when he appears?—There before me was a great multitude ... standing before the throne and in front of the Lamb. They were wearing white robes.... "They have washed their robes and made them white in the blood of the Lamb. Therefore, they are before the throne of God."

MALACHI 3:2; REVELATION 7:9, 14—15

June 28

"*I* KNOW THAT MY Redeemer lives."—Because Jesus lives forever, he has a permanent priesthood. Therefore he is able to save completely those who come to God through him, because he always lives to intercede for them.—"Because I live, you also will live."

JOB 19:25; HEBREWS 7:24—25; JOHN 14:19

June 29

*H*IS COMMANDMENTS ARE NOT burden-
some.—In my inner being I delight in
God's law.—This is his command: to
believe in the name of his Son, Jesus Christ,
and to love one another as he commanded
us.—Love is the fulfillment of the law.

1 JOHN 5:3; ROMANS 7:22; 1 JOHN 3:23; ROMANS 13:10

June 30

"*T*HOSE WHOM I LOVE I rebuke and discipline."—"My son, do not make light of
the Lord's discipline, and do not lose heart
when he rebukes you, because the Lord disciplines those he loves, and he punishes
everyone he accepts as a son."—The LORD
disciplines those he loves, as a father the
son he delights in.

REVELATION 3:19; HEBREWS 12:5–6; PROVERBS 3:12

July 1

*I*T IS BETTER TO take refuge in the LORD
than to trust in man. It is better to take
refuge in the LORD than to trust in princes.
Blessed is he whose help is the God of
Jacob, whose hope is in the LORD his
God.—"When I sent you without purse,
bag or sandals, did you lack anything?"
"Nothing," they answered.

PSALM 118:8–9; 146:5; LUKE 22:35

July 2

[*J*ESUS] PRAYED THE THIRD time, saying
the same thing.—During the days of Jesus'
life on earth, he offered up prayers and
petitions with loud cries and tears to the
one who could save him from death.—"Yet
not as I will, but as you will."

MATTHEW 26:44; HEBREWS 5:7; MATTHEW 26:39

July 3

*J*ESUS ... SAW TWO BROTHERS ... casting a
net into the lake, for they were fishermen.
"Come, follow me," Jesus said.—When
they saw the courage of Peter and John and
realized that they were unschooled, ordinary
men, they were astonished and they took
note that these men had been with Jesus.

MATTHEW 4:18–19; ACTS 4:13

July 4

"*A*S A MOTHER COMFORTS her child, so
will I comfort you."—"I will not leave you
as orphans; I will come to you."—"Can a
mother forget the baby at her breast and
have no compassion on the child she has
borne? Though she may forget, I will not
forget you!"

ISAIAH 66:13; JOHN 14:18; ISAIAH 49:15

July 5

*H*AS NOT GOD CHOSEN those who are poor in the eyes of the world to be rich in faith and to inherit the kingdom he promised those who love him?—God chose the foolish things of the world to shame the wise; God chose the weak things of the world to shame the strong.—My heart is not proud, O LORD.

JAMES 2:5; 1 CORINTHIANS 1:27; PSALM 131:1

July 6

*F*OR YOUR LOVE IS ever before me.—The LORD is gracious and compassionate, slow to anger and rich in love.—Be imitators of God, therefore, as dearly loved children and live a life of love, just as Christ loved us and gave himself up for us as a fragrant offering and sacrifice to God.

PSALM 26:3; 145:8; EPHESIANS 5:1–2

July 7

*N*O TEMPTATION HAS SEIZED you except what is common to man. And God is faithful; he will not let you be tempted beyond what you can bear. But when you are tempted, he will also provide a way out so that you can stand up under it.

1 CORINTHIANS 10:13

July 8

I KNOW MY TRANSGRESSIONS, and my sin is always before me. Against you, you only, have I sinned and done what is evil in your sight.—"I have swept away your offenses like a cloud, your sins like the morning mist. Return to me, for I have redeemed you."

PSALM 51:3–4; ISAIAH 44:22

July 9

O GREAT AND POWERFUL God, whose name is the Lord Almighty, great are your purposes and mighty are your deeds. Your eyes are open to all the ways of men; you reward everyone according to his conduct and as his deeds deserve.

JEREMIAH 32:18–19

July 10

*M*Y SON, GIVE ME your heart.—"Oh, that their hearts would be inclined to fear me and keep all my commands always, so that it might go well with them and their children forever!"—I run in the path of your commands, for you have set my heart free.

PROVERBS 23:26; DEUTERONOMY 5:29; PSALM 119:32

July 11

*C*AN PLUNDER BE TAKEN from warriors, or captives rescued from the fierce? But this is what the Lord says: "Yes, captives will be taken from warriors, and plunder retrieved from the fierce; I will contend with those who contend with you. . . . Then all mankind will know that I, the Lord, am your Savior, your Redeemer, the Mighty One of Jacob."

ISAIAH 49:24–26

July 12

*T*HE LORD GOD SAID, "It is not good for the man to be alone."—Two are better than one, because they have a good return for their work; if one falls down, his friend can help him up. But pity the man who falls and has no one to help him up!

GENESIS 2:18; ECCLESIASTES 4:9–10

July 13

"*F*IX THESE WORDS OF mine in your hearts and minds; tie them as symbols on your hands and bind them on your foreheads."—We have the word of the prophets made more certain, and you will do well to pay attention to it, as to a light shining in a dark place.

DEUTERONOMY 11:18; 2 PETER 1:19

July 14

O*H, THAT YOU WOULD* rend the heavens and come down.—When can I go and meet with God?—We wait for the blessed hope—the glorious appearing of our great God and Savior, Jesus Christ.—He who testifies to these things says, "Yes, I am coming soon." Amen. Come, Lord Jesus.

ISAIAH 64:1; PSALM 42:2; TITUS 2:13; REVELATION 22:20

July 15

"He calls his own sheep by name and leads them out. When he has brought out all his own, he goes on ahead of them, and his sheep follow him because they know his voice. But they will never follow a stranger; in fact, they will run away from him because they do not recognize a stranger's voice."

John 10:3–5

July 16

"You will be for me a kingdom of priests and a holy nation."—You are a chosen people, a royal priesthood, a holy nation, a people belonging to God, that you may declare the praises of him who called you out of darkness into his wonderful light.

Exodus 19:6; 1 Peter 2:9

July 17

*Y*OU ARE A GRACIOUS and compassionate God, slow to anger and abounding in love, a God who relents from sending calamity.— "The LORD is slow to anger, abounding in love and forgiving sin and rebellion."—May your mercy come quickly to meet us, for we are in desperate need.

JONAH 4:2; NUMBERS 14:18; PSALM 79:8

July 18

*L*ET US NOT LOVE with words or tongue but with actions and in truth.—Suppose a brother or sister is without clothes and daily food. If one of you says to him, "Go, I wish you well; keep warm and well fed," but does nothing about his physical needs, what good is it?

1 JOHN 3:18; JAMES 2:15–16

July 19

*F*OR THE MIGHTY ONE has done great things for me—holy is his name.—"Who among the gods is like you, O LORD? Who is like you—majestic in holiness, awesome in glory, working wonders?"—"Who will not fear you, O Lord, and bring glory to your name? For you alone are holy."— "... hallowed be your name..."

LUKE 1:49; EXODUS 15:11; REVELATION 15:4;

MATTHEW 6:9

July 20

*T*HOUGH THE FIG TREE does not bud and there are no grapes on the vines, though the olive crop fails and the fields produce no food, though there are no sheep in the pen and no cattle in the stalls, yet I will rejoice in the LORD, I will be joyful in God my Savior.

HABAKKUK 3:17–18

July 21

THE LORD JESUS, ON the night he was betrayed, took bread, and when he had given thanks, he broke it and said, "This is my body, which is for you; do this in remembrance of me."—"This bread is my flesh, which I will give for the life of the world."

1 CORINTHIANS 11:23–24; JOHN 6:51

July 22

THE DEATH HE DIED, he died to sin once for all; but the life he lives, he lives to God.—He who has suffered in his body is done with sin. As a result, he does not live the rest of his earthly life for evil human desires but rather for the will of God.

ROMANS 6:10; 1 PETER 4:1–2

July 23

"No one knows about that day or hour, not even the angels in heaven, nor the Son, but only the Father. Be on guard! Be alert!"—"Be dressed ready for service and keep your lamps burning, like men waiting for their master to return from a wedding banquet, so that when he comes and knocks they can immediately open the door for him."

Mark 13:32–33; Luke 12:35–36

July 24

He did not waver through unbelief regarding the promise of God.—He who had received the promises was about to sacrifice his one and only son, even though God had said to him, "It is through Isaac that your offspring will be reckoned." Abraham reasoned that God could raise the dead.— "Is anything too hard for the Lord?"

Romans 4:20; Hebrews 11:17–19; Genesis 18:14

July 25

"WHOEVER HEARS MY WORD and believes him who sent me has eternal life and will not be condemned; he has crossed over from death to life."—For he has rescued us from the dominion of darkness and brought us into the kingdom of the Son he loves.

JOHN 5:24; COLOSSIANS 1:13

July 26

GOD'S TEMPLE IS SACRED, and you are that temple.—What kind of people ought you to be? You ought to live holy and godly lives.—Do not let any unwholesome talk come out of your mouths.... And do not grieve the Holy Spirit of God.

1 CORINTHIANS 3:17; 2 PETER 3:11; EPHESIANS 4:29–30

July 27

NO KING IS SAVED by the size of his army; no warrior escapes by his great strength. A horse is a vain hope for deliverance; despite all its great strength it cannot save.—For our struggle is not against flesh and blood.... Therefore put on the full armor of God.

PSALM 33:16–17; EPHESIANS 6:12–13

July 28

"A NEW COMMAND I give you: Love one another. As I have loved you, so you must love one another."—Above all, love each other deeply, because love covers over a multitude of sins.—Love covers over all wrongs.—Live a life of love.

JOHN 13:34; 1 PETER 4:8; PROVERBS 10:12;

EPHESIANS 5:2

July 29

THE LIONS MAY GROW weak and hungry, but those who seek the Lord lack no good thing.—For you who revere my name, the sun of righteousness will rise with healing in its wings. And you will go out and leap like calves released from the stall.

PSALM 34:10; MALACHI 4:2

July 30

MANY EVEN AMONG THE leaders believed in him. But because of the Pharisees they would not confess their faith for fear they would be put out of the synagogue; for they loved praise from men more than praise from God.—"Whoever acknowledges me before men, I will also acknowledge him before my Father in heaven."

JOHN 12:42–43; MATTHEW 10:32

July 31

THERE IS ONE BODY and one Spirit.... You are no longer foreigners and aliens, but fellow citizens with God's people and members of God's household.—How good and pleasant it is when brothers live together in unity! It is like precious oil poured on the head, running down on the beard, running down on Aaron's beard, down upon the collar of his robes.

EPHESIANS 4:4; 2:19; PSALM 133:1–2

August 1

WE LIVE BY FAITH, not by sight.— Though you have not seen him, you love him; and even though you do not see him now, you believe in him and are filled with an inexpressible and glorious joy, for you are receiving the goal of your faith, the salvation of your souls.

2 CORINTHIANS 5:7; 1 PETER 1:8–9

August 2

"*T*HEY ARE TO TAKE some of the blood and put it on the sides and tops of the doorframes of the houses where they eat the lambs.... When I see the blood, I will pass over you."—Christ, our Passover lamb, has been sacrificed.—In him we have redemption through his blood.

EXODUS 12:7, 13; 1 CORINTHIANS 5:7; EPHESIANS 1:7

August 3

*T*HE LORD IS NEAR to all who call on him, to all who call on him in truth. He fulfills the desires of those who fear him; he hears their cry and saves them.... The Lord is close to the brokenhearted and saves those who are crushed in spirit.

PSALM 145:18–19; 34:18

August 4

DAY AFTER DAY EVERY priest stands and performs his religious duties; again and again he offers the same sacrifices, which can never take away sins. But when this priest had offered for all time one sacrifice for sins, he sat down at the right hand of God.... By one sacrifice he has made perfect forever those who are being made holy.

HEBREWS 10:11–12, 14

August 5

I HAVE STILLED AND quieted my soul; like a weaned child with its mother, like a weaned child is my soul within me.—I would like you to be free from concern.— You will keep in perfect peace him whose mind is steadfast, because he trusts in you.

PSALM 131:2; 1 CORINTHIANS 7:32; ISAIAH 26:3

August 6

*T*HE EARTH IS THE Lord's, and everything
in it.—God... richly provides us with
everything for our enjoyment.... For everything God created is good, and nothing is
to be rejected if it is received with thanksgiving, because it is consecrated by the word
of God and prayer.

PSALM 24:1; 1 TIMOTHY 6:17; 4:4–5

August 7

*L*IFT UP YOUR HEADS, O you gates; lift
them up, you ancient doors, that the King
of glory may come in. Who is he, this King
of glory? The LORD Almighty—he is the
King of glory.—On his robe and on his
thigh he has this name written: KING OF
KINGS AND LORD OF LORDS.

PSALM 24:9–10; REVELATION 19:16

August 8

*N*OT THAT I HAVE already obtained all this, or have already been made perfect, but I press on to take hold of that for which Christ Jesus took hold of me.—We, who with unveiled faces all reflect the Lord's glory, are being transformed into his likeness with ever-increasing glory.

PHILIPPIANS 3:12; 2 CORINTHIANS 3:18

August 9

I undertook great projects: I built houses for myself and planted vineyards.... I amassed silver and gold for myself.... Yet when I surveyed all that my hands had done and what I had toiled to achieve, everything was meaningless.—"If a man is thirsty, let him come to me and drink."

ECCLESIASTES 2:4, 8, 11; JOHN 7:37

August 10

[B]E] BLAMELESS AND PURE, children of
God without fault in a crooked and
depraved generation, in which you shine like
stars in the universe.—"You are the salt of
the earth.... You are the light of the
world.... Let your light shine before men,
that they may see your good deeds and
praise your Father in heaven."

PHILIPPIANS 2:15; MATTHEW 5:13–14, 16

August 11

[G]OD IS LIGHT; in him there is no darkness
at all. If we claim to have fellowship with
him yet walk in the darkness, we lie and do
not live by the truth. But if we walk in the
light, as he is in the light, we have fellowship with one another, and the blood of
Jesus, his Son, purifies us from every sin.

1 JOHN 1:5–7

August 12

"BUT LORD," GIDEON ASKED, "how can I save Israel? My clan is the weakest in Manasseh, and I am the least in my family."—"Not by might nor by power, but by my Spirit," says the Lord Almighty.—Be strong in the Lord and in his mighty power.

JUDGES 6:15; ZECHARIAH 4:6; EPHESIANS 6:10

August 13

YOU WERE WASHED, YOU were sanctified, you were justified in the name of the Lord Jesus Christ and by the Spirit of our God.—He saved us through the washing of rebirth and renewal by the Holy Spirit, whom he poured out on us generously through Jesus Christ our Savior.

1 CORINTHIANS 6:11; TITUS 3:5–6

August 14

SHOUT FOR JOY, O heavens; rejoice, O earth; burst into song, O mountains!... My soul rejoices in my God. For he has clothed me with garments of salvation and arrayed me in a robe of righteousness, as a bridegroom adorns his head like a priest, and as a bride adorns herself with her jewels.

ISAIAH 49:13; 61:10

August 15

EVERY GOOD AND PERFECT gift is from above, coming down from the Father.— Then you will be able to test and approve what God's will is—his good, pleasing and perfect will.—Filled with the fruit of righteousness that comes through Jesus Christ.

JAMES 1:17; ROMANS 12:2; PHILIPPIANS 1:11

August 16

"*I* WAS THERE WHEN he set the heavens in place, when he marked out the horizon on the face of the deep, when he established the clouds above and fixed securely the fountains of the deep, when he gave the sea its boundary so the waters would not overstep his command, and when he marked out the foundations of the earth."

PROVERBS 8:27–29

August 17

"*T*HE GRASS WITHERS AND the flowers fall, because the breath of the LORD blows on them. Surely the people are grass. The grass withers and the flowers fall, but the word of our God stands forever."—The world and its desires pass away, but the man who does the will of God lives forever.

ISAIAH 40:7–8; 1 JOHN 2:17

August 18

"LET NOT THE WISE man boast of his wisdom or the strong man boast of his strength or the rich man boast of his riches, but let him who boasts boast about this: that he understands and knows me, that I am the LORD."—NOT TO US, O Lord, not to us but to your name be the glory.

JEREMIAH 9:23–24; PSALM 115:1

August 19

JUST AS HE WHO called you is holy, so be holy in all you do.—We dealt with each of you . . . urging you to live lives worthy of God, who calls you into his kingdom and glory.—So whether you eat or drink or whatever you do, do it all for the glory of God.

1 PETER 1:15; 1 THESSALONIANS 2:11–12;

1 CORINTHIANS 10:31

August 20

GOD IS NOT A MAN, that he should lie, nor a son of man, that he should change his mind.—The Father of the heavenly lights, who does not change like shifting shadows.—Jesus Christ is the same yesterday and today and forever.—The faithful God, keeping his covenant of love to a thousand generations.

NUMBERS 23:19; JAMES 1:17; HEBREWS 13:8;

DEUTERONOMY 7:9

August 21

GOD PLACED ALL THINGS under his feet and appointed him to be head over everything for the church.... Christ loved the church and gave himself up for her ... to present her to himself as a radiant church, without stain or wrinkle or any other blemish, but holy and blameless.

EPHESIANS 1:22; 5:25, 27

August 22

*V*ERY RARELY WILL ANYONE die for a righteous man, though for a good man someone might possibly dare to die. But God demonstrates his own love for us in this: While we were still sinners, Christ died for us.—He humbled himself and became obedient to death—even death on a cross!—This love . . . surpasses knowledge.

ROMANS 5:7–8; PHILIPPIANS 2:8; EPHESIANS 3:19

August 23

*F*ROM THE BEGINNING GOD chose you to be saved through the sanctifying work of the Spirit and through belief in the truth.—This grace was given us in Christ Jesus before the beginning of time.—All the days ordained for me were written in your book before one of them came to be.

2 THESSALONIANS 2:13; 2 TIMOTHY 1:9; PSALM 139:16

August 24

"*I* HAVE INDEED SEEN the misery of my people."—When Jesus saw her weeping, and the Jews who had come along with her also weeping, he was deeply moved in spirit and troubled. . . . Jesus wept.—In all their distress he too was distressed, and the angel of his presence saved them.

EXODUS 3:7; JOHN 11:33, 35; ISAIAH 63:9

August 25

*S*ING AND MAKE MUSIC in your heart to the Lord, always giving thanks to God the Father for everything.—About midnight Paul and Silas were praying and singing hymns to God, and the other prisoners were listening to them.—Rejoice in the Lord always. I will say it again: Rejoice!

EPHESIANS 5:19–20; ACTS 16:25; PHILIPPIANS 4:4

August 26

...*M*Y CUP OVERFLOWS.—TASTE AND see
that the LORD is good; blessed is the man
who takes refuge in him. Fear the Lord, you
his saints, for those who fear him lack nothing.—His compassions never fail. They are
new every morning; great is your faithfulness.

PSALM 23:5; 34:8–9; LAMENTATIONS 3:22–23

August 27

*B*Y THE WORD OF your lips I have kept
myself from the ways of the violent. My
steps have held to your paths; my feet have
not slipped.—When you walk, they will
guide you; when you sleep, they will watch
over you; when you awake, they will speak
to you. For these commands are a lamp,
this teaching is a light.

PSALM 17:4–5; PROVERBS 6:22–23

August 28

GOD HAS GIVEN US eternal life, and this life is in his Son.—"He gave his one and only Son, that whoever believes in him shall not perish but have eternal life."—"To him who overcomes, I will give the right to eat from the tree of life, which is in the paradise of God."

1 JOHN 5:11; JOHN 3:16; REVELATION 2:7

August 29

HE WILL COVER YOU with his feathers, and under his wings you will find refuge.—"As a hen gathers her chicks under her wings."—I long to dwell in your tent forever and take refuge in the shelter of your wings.—I will trust and not be afraid.

PSALM 91:4; MATTHEW 23:37; PSALM 61:4; ISAIAH 12:2

August 30

"*T*HE BREAD OF GOD is he who comes down from heaven and gives life to the world." ... "Your forefathers ate the manna in the desert, yet they died.... If a man eats of this bread, he will live forever.... My flesh is real food and my blood is real drink."

JOHN 6:33, 49, 51, 55

August 31

*T*HE GIFT FOLLOWED MANY trespasses and brought justification.... But the gift is not like the trespass. For if the many died by the trespass of the one man, how much more did God's grace and the gift that came by the grace of the one man, Jesus Christ, overflow to the many!

ROMANS 5:16, 15

September 1

*"I*F ANYONE WOULD COME after me, he must deny himself and take up his cross daily and follow me."—Everyone who wants to live a godly life in Christ Jesus will be persecuted.—If you suffer as a Christian, do not be ashamed, but praise God that you bear that name.

LUKE 9:23; 2 TIMOTHY 3:12; 1 PETER 4:16

September 2

*H*E MAKES ME LIE down in green pastures.—I delight to sit in his shade, and his fruit is sweet to my taste. He has taken me to the banquet hall, and his banner over me is love.

PSALM 23:2; SONG OF SONGS 2:3–4

September 3

I AM AFRAID THAT just as Eve was deceived by the serpent's cunning, your minds may somehow be led astray from your sincere and pure devotion to Christ.—Take the helmet of salvation and the sword of the Spirit, which is the word of God.—In order that Satan might not outwit us.

2 CORINTHIANS 11:3; EPHESIANS 6:17;

2 CORINTHIANS 2:11

September 4

*"B*E STILL, AND KNOW that I am God."— Mary . . . sat at the Lord's feet listening to what he said.—"In repentance and rest is your salvation, in quietness and trust is your strength."—Search your hearts and be silent. . . . Be still before the Lord and wait patiently for him.

PSALM 46:10; LUKE 10:39; ISAIAH 30:15; PSALM 4:4; 37:7

September 5

"WHOEVER DRINKS THE WATER I give him will never thirst. Indeed, the water I give him will become in him a spring of water welling up to eternal life."—Whoever is thirsty, let him come; and whoever wishes, let him take the free gift of the water of life.

JOHN 4:14; REVELATION 22:17

September 6

LET US LIFT UP our hearts and our hands to God in heaven.—Show me the way I should go, for to you I lift up my soul.—I will praise you as long as I live, and in your name I will lift up my hands.—Bring joy to your servant, for to you, O LORD, I lift up my soul.

LAMENTATIONS 3:41; PSALM 143:8; 63:4; 86:4

September 7

*I*F ONLY FOR THIS life we have hope in Christ, we are to be pitied more than all men.—Praise be to the God and Father of our Lord Jesus Christ! In his great mercy he has given us new birth into a living hope through the resurrection of Jesus Christ from the dead.

1 CORINTHIANS 15:19; 1 PETER 1:3

September 8

*G*OD CANNOT BE MOCKED. A man reaps what he sows. The one who sows to please his sinful nature, from that nature will reap destruction; the one who sows to please the Spirit, from the Spirit will reap eternal life.—"What good will it be for a man if he gains the whole world, yet forfeits his soul?"

GALATIANS 6:7–8; MATTHEW 16:26

September 9

"MY FOOT IS SLIPPING."—THOUGH a righteous man falls seven times, he rises again.—Do not gloat over me, my enemy! Though I have fallen, I will rise. Though I sit in darkness, the LORD will be my light.—If anybody does sin, we have one who speaks to the Father in our defense—Jesus Christ, the Righteous One.

PSALM 94:18; PROVERBS 24:16; MICAH 7:8; 1 JOHN 2:1

September 10

"YOU COME AGAINST ME with sword and spear and javelin, but I come against you in the name of the Lord Almighty."— Contend, O Lord, with those who contend with me; fight against those who fight against me. Take up shield and buckler; arise and come to my aid.

1 SAMUEL 17:45; PSALM 35:1–2

September 11

"*D*O NOT FOLLOW THE crowd in doing wrong."—Don't you know that friendship with the world is hatred toward God? Anyone who chooses to be a friend of the world becomes an enemy of God.—For what do righteousness and wickedness have in common? Or what fellowship can light have with darkness?

EXODUS 23:2; JAMES 4:4; 2 CORINTHIANS 6:14

September 12

O LORD, YOU HAVE searched me and you know me. You know when I sit and when I rise; you perceive my thoughts from afar. You discern my going out and my lying down; you are familiar with all my ways.— Everything is uncovered and laid bare before the eyes of him to whom we must give account.

PSALM 139:1–3; HEBREWS 4:13

September 13

*Y*OU HAVE BEEN BORN again, not of perishable seed, but of imperishable, through the living and enduring word of God.— "He who believes in me will live, even though he dies; and whoever lives and believes in me will never die."—The body that is sown is perishable, it is raised imperishable.

1 PETER 1:23; JOHN 11:25–26; 1 CORINTHIANS 15:42

September 14

*G*OD ... HAS CALLED YOU into fellowship with his Son.—For he received honor and glory from God the Father when the voice came to him from the Majestic Glory, saying, "This is my Son, whom I love."—How great is the love the Father has lavished on us, that we should be called children of God!

1 CORINTHIANS 1:9; 2 PETER 1:17; 1 JOHN 3:1

September 15

*H*E IS A DOUBLE-MINDED man, unstable in all he does.—"No one who puts his hand to the plow and looks back is fit for service in the kingdom of God."—Always give yourselves fully to the work of the Lord, because you know that your labor in the Lord is not in vain.

JAMES 1:8; LUKE 9:62; 1 CORINTHIANS 15:58

September 16

*T*HE LORD WEIGHS THE HEART.—"Then your Father, who sees what is done in secret, will reward you."—Search me, O God, and know my heart; test me and know my anxious thoughts. See if there is any offensive way in me, and lead me in the way everlasting.

PROVERBS 21:2; MATTHEW 6:4; PSALM 139:23–24

September 17

THE MASTER OF THE banquet tasted the water that had been turned into wine. He did not realize where it had come from... and said, "Everyone brings out the choice wine first and then the cheaper wine after the guests have had too much to drink; but you have saved the best till now."

JOHN 2:9–10

September 18

OH, THE DEPTH OF the riches of the wisdom and knowledge of God! How unsearchable his judgments, and his paths beyond tracing out! "Who has known the mind of the Lord? Or who has been his counselor?" ... From him and through him and to him are all things.

ROMANS 11:33–34, 36

September 19

I LIFT UP MY EYES TO THE HILLS—where does my help come from? My help comes from the LORD.... AS THE MOUNTAINS SURROUND JERUSALEM, SO THE Lord surrounds his people both now and forevermore.... I lift up my eyes to you, to you whose throne is in heaven.

PSALM 121:1–2; 125:2; 123:1

September 20

*P*OOR, YET MAKING MANY rich.... You know the grace of our Lord Jesus Christ, that though he was rich, yet for your sakes he became poor, so that you through his poverty might become rich.—From the fullness of his grace we have all received one blessing after another.

2 CORINTHIANS 6:10; 8:9; JOHN 1:16

September 21

"*H*E WILL GIVE YOU another Counselor to be with you forever—the Spirit of truth. The world cannot accept him, because it neither sees him nor knows him. But you know him, for he lives with you and will be in you."—"He will bring glory to me by taking from what is mine and making it known to you."

September 22

*M*Y LOVER IS . . . OUTSTANDING among ten thousand.—The ruler of the kings of the earth.—His head is purest gold.—He is the head of the body, the church.—His lips are like lilies dripping with myrrh.— "No one ever spoke the way this man does."

SONG OF SONGS 5:10; REVELATION 1:5; SONG OF SONGS 5:11; COLOSSIANS 1:18; SONG OF SONGS 5:13; JOHN 7:46

September 23

*T*HEY WERE LONGING FOR a better country—a heavenly one. Therefore God is not ashamed to be called their God, for he has prepared a city for them.—An inheritance that can never perish, spoil or fade.—"No eye has seen, no ear has heard, no mind has conceived what God has prepared for those who love him."

HEBREWS 11:16; 1 PETER 1:4; 1 CORINTHIANS 2:9

September 24

*A*S FOR ME, IT is good to be near God.—Better is one day in your courts than a thousand elsewhere; I would rather be a doorkeeper in the house of my God than dwell in the tents of the wicked.—Blessed are those you choose and bring near to live in your courts!

PSALM 73:28; 84:10; 65:4

September 25

GOD WILL JUDGE MEN'S secrets through Jesus Christ.—Judge nothing before the appointed time; wait till the Lord comes. He will bring to light what is hidden in darkness and will expose the motives of men's hearts.—"The Father judges no one, but has entrusted all judgment to the Son."

ROMANS 2:16; 1 CORINTHIANS 4:5; JOHN 5:22

September 26

WE MUST ALL APPEAR before the judgment seat of Christ, that each one may receive what is due him for the things done while in the body, whether good or bad.—Mercy triumphs over judgment!—For the wages of sin is death, but the gift of God is eternal life in Christ Jesus our Lord.

2 CORINTHIANS 5:10; JAMES 2:13; ROMANS 6:23

September 27

*T*HE TEMPTER CAME TO him and said, "If you are the Son of God tell these stones to become bread." Jesus answered, "It is written man does not live on bread alone, but on every word that comes from the mouth of God." Then the devil left him.—I have hidden your word in my heart that I might not sin against you.

MATTHEW 4:3–4; PSALM 119:11

September 28

*T*HE SUN HAS ONE kind of splendor, the moon another and the stars another; and star differs from star in splendor. So will it be with the resurrection of the dead.— Those who are wise will shine like the brightness of the heavens, and those who lead many to righteousness, like the stars for ever and ever.

1 CORINTHIANS 15:41–42; DANIEL 12:3

September 29

*T*HE LORD GIVES WISDOM, and from his mouth come knowledge and understanding.—"I will give you words and wisdom that none of your adversaries will be able to resist or contradict."—"I, even I, am the LORD, and apart from me there is no savior."

PROVERBS 2:6; LUKE 21:15; ISAIAH 43:11

September 30

*I*N A LARGE HOUSE there are articles not only of gold and silver, but also of wood and clay; some are for noble purposes and some for ignoble. If a man cleanses himself from the latter, he will be an instrument for noble purposes, made holy, useful to the Master and prepared to do any good work.

2 TIMOTHY 2:20—21

October 1

*L*ET US NOT BE like others, who are asleep, but let us be alert and self-controlled.—Say "No" to ungodliness and worldly passions, and . . . live self-controlled, upright and godly lives in this present age, while we wait for the blessed hope—the glorious appearing of our great God and Savior, Jesus Christ.

1 THESSALONIANS 5:6; TITUS 2:12–13

October 2

"*T*HE GOAT WILL CARRY on itself all their sins to a solitary place."—As far as the east is from the west, so far has he removed our transgressions from us.—"In those days, at that time," declares the Lord, "search will be made for Israel's guilt, but there will be none."

LEVITICUS 16:22; PSALM 103:12; JEREMIAH 50:20

October 3

*H*E HIMSELF BORE OUR sins in his body on the tree, so that we might die to sins and live for righteousness; by his wounds you have been healed.—I urge you, brothers, in view of God's mercy, to offer your bodies as living sacrifices, holy and pleasing to God.

1 PETER 2:24; ROMANS 12:1

October 4

*H*IS FACE WAS RADIANT because he had spoken with the LORD.—[Jesus] was transfigured before them. His face shone like the sun, and his clothes became as white as the light.—All who were sitting in the Sanhedrin looked intently at Stephen, and they saw that his face was like the face of an angel.

EXODUS 34:29; MATTHEW 17:2; ACTS 6:15

October 5

I LOVE THE LORD, for he heard my voice;
he heard my cry for mercy. Because he
turned his ear to me, I will call on him as
long as I live. The cords of death entangled
me, the anguish of the grave came upon
me; I was overcome by trouble and sorrow.
Then I called on the name of the Lord.

PSALM 116:1–4

October 6

*L*ORD GOD ALMIGHTY REIGNS.—"I know
that you can do all things."—"What is
impossible with men is possible with
God."—"Lord, if you are willing, you can
make me clean." Jesus reached out his hand
and touched the man. "I am willing," he
said. "Be clean!"

REVELATION 19:6; JOB 42:2; LUKE 18:27;

MATTHEW 8:2–3

October 7

"*I*T IS MORE BLESSED to give than to receive."—"When you give a banquet, invite the poor, the crippled, the lame, the blind, and you will be blessed. Although they cannot repay you, you will be repaid at the resurrection of the righteous."— Blessed is he who has regard for the weak.

ACTS 20:35; LUKE 14:13–14; PSALM 41:1

October 8

*H*E SET MY FEET ON A ROCK.—That rock was Christ.—Simon Peter answered, "You are the Christ, the Son of the living God."— "Salvation is found in no one else, for there is no other name under heaven given to men by which we must be saved."

PSALM 40:2; 1 CORINTHIANS 10:4; MATTHEW 16:16;

ACTS 4:12

October 9

"*E*VERYTHING THAT WAS WRITTEN in the past was written to teach us, so that through endurance and the encouragement of the Scriptures we might have hope."—Your promises have been thoroughly tested, and your servant loves them.—"Every word of God is flawless."—I meditate on your precepts and consider your ways.

ROMANS 15:4; PSALM 119:140, PROVERBS 30:5;
PSALM 119:15

October 10

*Y*OU ARE ALL SONS of God through faith in Christ Jesus.... Because you are sons, God sent the Spirit of his Son into our hearts, the Spirit who calls out, *"Abba, Father."*—"I will be a Father to you, and you will be my sons and daughters, says the Lord."

GALATIANS 3:26; 4:6; 2 CORINTHIANS 6:18

October 11

"...*H*ALLOWED BE YOUR NAME."—I saw the LORD seated on a throne, high and exalted, and the train of his robe filled the temple. Above him were seraphs.... And they were calling to one another: "Holy, holy, holy is the LORD Almighty; the whole earth is full of his glory."

MATTHEW 6:9; ISAIAH 6:1–3

October 12

"*Y*OUR KINGDOM COME..."—"IN THE time of those kings, the God of heaven will set up a kingdom that will never be destroyed, nor will it be left to another people. It will crush all those kingdoms and bring them to an end, but it will itself endure forever."

MATTHEW 6:10; DANIEL 2:44

October 13

"*Y*OUR WILL BE DONE on earth as it is in heaven."—It is God's will that you should be sanctified.—He does not live the rest of his earthly life for evil human desires, but rather for the will of God.—"Whoever does God's will is my brother and sister and mother."

MATTHEW 6:10; 1 THESSALONIANS 4:3; 1 PETER 4:2;
MARK 3:35

October 14

"*G*IVE US TODAY OUR daily bread." —He humbled you, causing you to hunger and then feeding you with manna, which neither you nor your fathers had known, to teach you that man does not live on bread alone but on every word that comes from the mouth of the LORD.

MATTHEW 6:11; DEUTERONOMY 8:3

October 15

"*F*ORGIVE US OUR DEBTS, as we also have forgiven our debtors...."—"You wicked servant," he said, "I canceled all that debt of yours because you begged me to. Shouldn't you have had mercy on your fellow servant just as I had on you?"—Forgive as the Lord forgave you.

MATTHEW 6:12; 18:32–33; COLOSSIANS 3:13

October 16

"*A*ND LEAD US NOT into temptation, but deliver us from the evil one...."—When tempted, no one should say, "God is tempting me." For God cannot be tempted by evil, nor does he tempt anyone; but each one is tempted when, by his own evil desire, he is dragged away and enticed.—"Come out from them and be separate."

MATTHEW 6:13; JAMES 1:13–14; 2 CORINTHIANS 6:17

October 17

"*H*E WILL REIGN OVER the house of Jacob forever; his kingdom will never end."—Not to us, O LORD, not to us but to your name be the glory.—Yours, O LORD, is the greatness and the power and the glory and the majesty and the splendor, for everything in heaven and earth is yours. Yours, O LORD, is the kingdom.

LUKE 1:33; PSALM 115:1; 1 CHRONICLES 29:11

October 18

"*A*MEN! MAY THE Lord, the God of my lord the king, so declare it."—Praise be to the LORD God, the God of Israel, who alone does marvelous deeds. Praise be to his glorious name forever; may the whole earth be filled with his glory. Amen and Amen.

MATTHEW 6:13; 1 KINGS 1:36; PSALM 72:18–19

October 19

"MAN BORN OF WOMAN is of few days and full of trouble. He springs up like a flower and withers away; like a fleeting shadow, he does not endure."—We believe that Jesus died and rose again and so we believe that God will bring with Jesus those who have fallen asleep in him.

JOB 14:1–2; 1 THESSALONIANS 4:14

October 20

DO NOT MERELY LISTEN to the word, and so deceive yourselves. Do what it says. Anyone who listens to the word but does not do what it says is like a man who looks at his face in a mirror and . . . goes away and immediately forgets what he looks like.

JAMES 1:22–24

October 21

A DISPUTE AROSE AMONG them as to which of them was considered to be greatest.—[Jesus] got up from the meal, took off his outer clothing, and wrapped a towel around his waist. After that, he poured water into a basin and began to wash his disciples' feet, drying them with the towel that was wrapped around him.

LUKE 22:24; JOHN 13:4–5

October 22

*T*HE LOT IS CAST into the lap, but its every decision is from the Lord.—"I am the Lord, and there is no other; apart from me there is no God.... I form the light and create darkness, I bring prosperity and create disaster; I, the Lord, do all these things."

PROVERBS 16:33; ISAIAH 45:5, 7

October 23

"*A* MAN'S LIFE DOES not consist in the abundance of his possessions."—Better the little that the righteous have than the wealth of many wicked.—Keep your lives free from the love of money and be content with what you have, because God has said, "Never will I leave you; never will I forsake you."

LUKE 12:15; PSALM 37:16; HEBREWS 13:5

October 24

"*T*HE POOR AND NEEDY search for water, but there is none; their tongues are parched with thirst."—"They have forsaken me, the spring of living water, and have dug their own cisterns, broken cisterns that cannot hold water."—"Blessed are those who hunger and thirst for righteousness, for they will be filled."

ISAIAH 41:17; JEREMIAH 2:13; MATTHEW 5:6

October 25

GOD IS OUR REFUGE and strength, an ever-present help in trouble. Therefore we will not fear, though the earth give way and the mountains fall into the heart of the sea, though its waters roar and foam and the mountains quake with their surging.— "You will hear of wars and rumors of wars, but see to it that you are not alarmed."

PSALM 46:1–3; MATTHEW 24:6

October 26

"ARE NOT TWO SPARROWS sold for a penny? Yet not one of them will fall to the ground apart from the will of your Father. And even the very hairs of your head are all numbered. So don't be afraid; you are worth more than many sparrows."

MATTHEW 10:29–31

October 27

"BLESSED ARE THE POOR in spirit.... Blessed are those who mourn.... Blessed are the meek.... Blessed are those who hunger and thirst for righteousness.... Blessed are the merciful.... Blessed are the pure in heart.... Blessed are the peacemakers.... Blessed are those who are persecuted because of righteousness."—"Blessed... are those who hear the word of God and obey it."

MATTHEW 5:3–10; LUKE 11:28

October 28

"I LAY DOWN MY LIFE—only to take it up again. No one takes it from me, but I lay it down of my own accord. I have authority to lay it down and authority to take it up again."—"Turn to me and be saved, all you ends of the earth."

JOHN 10:17–18; ISAIAH 45:22

October 29

STAND FIRM THEN, WITH the belt of truth buckled around your waist, with the breast-plate of righteousness in place, and with your feet fitted with the readiness that comes from the gospel of peace. In addition to all this, take up the shield of faith, with which you can extinguish all the flaming arrows of the evil one.

EPHESIANS 6:14–16

October 30

YOU WILL NOT HAVE to fight this battle. Take up your positions; stand firm and see the deliverance the Lord will give you.— The battle is not yours, but God's.—It is not by sword or spear that the LORD saves; for the battle is the LORD's.

2 CHRONICLES 20:17, 15; 1 SAMUEL 17:47

October 31

I TRUST IN YOUR word.... Your decrees are
the theme of my song wherever I lodge....
The law from your mouth is more precious
to me than thousands of pieces of silver
and gold.... Your word, O LORD, is eternal;
it stands firm in the heavens. Your faithfulness continues through all generations.

PSALM 119:42, 54, 72, 89–90

November 1

*B*LESSED IS THE MAN who listens to me,
watching daily at my doors, waiting at my
doorway.—As the eyes of slaves look to
the hand of their master, as the eyes of a
maid look to the hand of her mistress, so
our eyes look to the LORD our God, till he
shows us his mercy.

PROVERBS 8:34; PSALM 123:2

November 2

"*H*E COMMITTED NO SIN, and no deceit was found in his mouth."—Let us throw off everything that hinders and the sin that so easily entangles.—Whatever is true, whatever is noble, whatever is right, whatever is pure, whatever is lovely, whatever is admirable—if anything is excellent or praiseworthy—think about such things.

1 PETER 2:22; HEBREWS 12:1; PHILIPPIANS 4:8

November 3

"*I* AND THE FATHER ARE ONE." ... "If you knew me, you would know my Father also." ... "Anyone who has seen me has seen the Father." ... "Before Abraham was born, I am!"—God said to Moses, "I am who I am. This is what you are to say to the Israelites: "I am has sent me to you."

JOHN 10:30; 8:19; 14:9; 8:58; EXODUS 3:14

November 4

*H*E WILL ENDURE AS long as the sun, as long as the moon, through all generations. He will be like rain falling on a mown field, like showers watering the earth. In his days the righteous will flourish; prosperity will abound till the moon is no more.—"Glory to God in the highest, and on earth peace to men."

PSALM 72:5–7; LUKE 2:14

November 5

"*G*OD ANOINTED JESUS OF Nazareth with the Holy Spirit and power."—God ... anointed us, set his seal of ownership on us, and put his Spirit in our hearts.—The fruit of the Spirit is love, joy, peace, patience, kindness, goodness, faithfulness, gentleness and self-control.

ACTS 10:38; 2 CORINTHIANS 1:21–22;

GALATIANS 5:22–23

November 6

*A*LL SCRIPTURE IS GOD-BREATHED and is useful for teaching, rebuking, correcting and training in righteousness, so that the man of God may be thoroughly equipped for every good work.... The holy Scriptures ... are able to make you wise for salvation through faith in Christ Jesus.

2 TIMOTHY 3:16–17, 15

November 7

*L*ET THEM GIVE THANKS to the LORD for his unfailing love and his wonderful deeds for men.—All you have made will praise you, O LORD; your saints will extol you. They will tell of the glory of your kingdom and speak of your might, so that all men may know of your mighty acts and the glorious splendor of your kingdom.

PSALM 107:8; 145:10–12

November 8

THE ISRAELITES CAMPED OPPOSITE them
like two small flocks of goats, while the
Arameans covered the countryside....
"This is what the Lord says: 'Because
the Arameans think the Lord is a god of
the hills and not a god of the valleys, I will
deliver this vast army into your hands, and
you will know that I am the Lord.'"

1 KINGS 20:27–28

November 9

"HE WILL SEND HIS angels and gather his
elect from the four winds, from the ends of
the earth to the ends of the heavens."—
Even if you have been banished to the most
distant land under the heavens, from there
the LORD your God will gather you and
bring you back.

MARK 13:27; DEUTERONOMY 30:4

November 10

DO NOT CONFORM ANY longer to the pattern of this world, but be transformed by the renewing of your mind.... Just as you used to offer the parts of your body in slavery to impurity and to ever-increasing wickedness, so now offer them in slavery to righteousness leading to holiness.

ROMANS 12:2; 6:19

November 11

"I AM SENDING AN angel ahead of you to guard you along the way and to bring you to the place I have prepared."—Lead me, O LORD, in your righteousness ... make straight your way before me.—Send forth your light and your truth, let them guide me; let them bring me to your holy mountain, to the place where you dwell.

EXODUS 23:20; PSALM 5:8; 43:3

November 12

GODLY SORROW BRINGS REPENTANCE that leads to salvation and leaves no regret.— Then Peter remembered the word Jesus had spoken: "Before the rooster crows, you will disown me three times." And he went outside and wept bitterly.—The sacrifices of God are a broken spirit; a broken and contrite heart, O God, you will not despise.

2 CORINTHIANS 7:10; MATTHEW 26:75; PSALM 51:17

November 13

THE LAW OF THE Lord is perfect, reviving the soul. The statutes of the Lord are trustworthy, making wise the simple. The precepts of the Lord are right, giving joy to the heart. The commands of the Lord are radiant, giving light to the eyes.

PSALM 19:7–8

November 14

*T*HE PRIESTS WHO CARRIED the ark of the covenant of the Lord stood firm on dry ground in the middle of the Jordan, while all Israel passed by until the whole nation had completed the crossing on dry ground.—"When you pass through the waters, I will be with you; and when you pass through the rivers, they will not sweep over you."

JOSHUA 3:17; ISAIAH 43:2

November 15

I PRAY THAT YOU, being rooted and established in love, may have power, together with all the saints, to grasp how wide and long and high and deep is the love of Christ, and to know this love that surpasses knowledge—that you may be filled to the measure of all the fullness of God.

EPHESIANS 3:17–19

November 16

"SANCTIFY THEM BY THE truth; your word is truth."—Let the word of Christ dwell in you richly as you teach and admonish one another with all wisdom.—"If you hold to my teaching, you are really my disciples. Then you will know the truth, and the truth will set you free."

JOHN 17:17; COLOSSIANS 3:16; JOHN 8:31–32

November 17

HE WHO SOWS RIGHTEOUSNESS reaps a sure reward.—The one who sows to please the Spirit, from the Spirit will reap eternal life.—A generous man will prosper; he who refreshes others will himself be refreshed.—Whoever sows generously will also reap generously.

PROVERBS 11:18; GALATIANS 6:8; PROVERB 11:25;
2 CORINTHIANS 9:6

November 18

"*I* DID NOT BELIEVE these things until I came and saw with my own eyes. Indeed, not even half was told me."—"The Queen of the South ... came from the ends of the earth to listen to Solomon's wisdom, and now one greater than Solomon is here." I will be satisfied with seeing your likeness.

1 KINGS 10:7; MATTHEW 12:42; PSALM 17:15

November 19

I SAW A NEW heaven and a new earth, for the first heaven and the first earth had passed away.... And I heard a loud voice from the throne saying, "Now the dwelling of God is with men, and he will live with them. They will be his people, and God himself will be with them and be their God."

REVELATION 21:1, 3

November 20

*T*HOUGH I SIT IN DARKNESS, the LORD will be my light.—I will lead the blind by ways they have not known, along unfamiliar paths I will guide them; I will turn the darkness into light before them and make the rough places smooth.—The LORD is my light and my salvation.

MICAH 7:8; ISAIAH 42:16; PSALM 27:1

November 21

*L*ET THE WICKED FORSAKE his way and the evil man his thoughts. Let him turn to the LORD, and he will have mercy on him, and to our God, for he will freely pardon.— "Jesus, remember me when you come into your kingdom." Jesus answered him, "I tell you the truth, today you will be with me in paradise."

ISAIAH 55:7; LUKE 23:42–43

November 22

*P*RAY IN THE HOLY SPIRIT.—The Spirit helps us in our weakness. We do not know what we ought to pray for, but the Spirit himself intercedes for us with groans that words cannot express.—Pray in the Spirit on all occasions with all kinds of prayers and requests.

JUDE 20; ROMANS 8:26; EPHESIANS 6:18

November 23

*J*ESUS IMMEDIATELY SAID TO THEM: "Take courage! It is I. Don't be afraid."—"Why are you troubled, and why do doubts rise in your minds? Look at my hands and my feet. It is I myself! Touch me and see; a ghost does not have flesh and bones, as you see I have."

MATTHEW 14:27; LUKE 24:38–39

November 24

"NOT EVERYONE WHO SAYS TO ME, 'Lord, Lord,' will enter the kingdom of heaven, but only he who does the will of my Father."—If we claim to have fellowship with him yet walk in the darkness, we lie and do not live by the truth.... But if anyone obeys his word, God's love is truly made complete in him.

MATTHEW 7:21; 1 JOHN 1:6, 2:5

November 25

"EVERYONE WHO CALLS ON the name of the Lord will be saved."—[Manasseh] did much evil in the eyes of the LORD, provoking him to anger.—In his distress he sought the favor of the LORD his God and humbled himself greatly.... And when he prayed to him, the LORD was moved by his entreaty and listened to his plea.

ACTS 2:21; 2 KINGS 21:6; 2 CHRONICLES 33:12–13

November 26

THE LORD HAS ANOINTED me to preach good news to the poor. He has sent me to bind up the brokenhearted, to proclaim freedom for the captives and release from darkness for the prisoners, to proclaim the year of the Lord's favor and the day of vengeance of our God, to comfort all who mourn, and provide for those who grieve in Zion.

ISAIAH 61:1–3

November 27

THEN MOSES SAID, "Now show me your glory." ... "But," [the Lord] said, "you cannot see my face, for no one may see me and live."—No one has ever seen God, but God the One and Only, who is at the Father's side, has made him known.

EXODUS 33:18, 20; JOHN 1:18

November 28

*A*DD TO YOUR FAITH goodness; and to goodness, knowledge; and to knowledge, self-control; and to self-control, perseverance; and to perseverance, godliness; and to godliness, brotherly kindness; and to brotherly kindness, love. For if you possess these qualities in increasing measure, they will keep you from being ineffective and unproductive in your knowledge of our Lord Jesus Christ.

2 PETER 1:5–8

November 29

*W*AS NOT OUR ANCESTOR Abraham considered righteous for what he did when he offered his son Isaac on the altar?... A person is justified by what he does and not by faith alone.... The man who looks intently into the perfect law that gives freedom, and continues to do this, not forgetting what he has heard, but doing it—he will be blessed.

JAMES 2:21, 24; 1:25

November 30

WE ... REJOICE IN OUR sufferings.—Dear friends, do not be surprised at the painful trial you are suffering, as though something strange were happening to you. But rejoice that you participate in the sufferings of Christ.—The apostles left the Sanhedrin, rejoicing because they had been counted worthy of suffering disgrace for the Name.

ROMANS 5:3; 1 PETER 4:12–13; ACTS 5:41

December 1

HE WHO DWELLS IN the shelter of the Most High will rest in the shadow of the Almighty.—The LORD is your shade at your right hand; the sun will not harm you by day, nor the moon by night.—You have been ... a shelter from the storm and a shade from the heat.

PSALM 91:1; 121:5–6; ISAIAH 25:4

December 2

*Y*OU HAVE AN ANOINTING from the Holy One, and all of you know the truth.—The anointing you received from him remains in you.—"The Counselor, the Holy Spirit, whom the Father will send in my name, will teach you all things and will remind you of everything I have said to you."

1 JOHN 2:20, 27, JOHN 14:26

December 3

*C*AST ALL YOUR ANXIETY on him because he cares for you.—Hezekiah received the letter from the messengers and read it. Then he went up to the temple of the LORD and spread it out before the LORD. And Hezekiah prayed to the LORD.—"Before they call I will answer; while they are still speaking I will hear."

1 PETER 5:7; ISAIAH 37:14–15; 65:24

December 4

"*A*H, SOVEREIGN Lord," I said, "I do not know how to speak; I am only a child." But the LORD said to me, "Do not say, 'I am only a child.' You must go to everyone I send you to and say whatever I command you. Do not be afraid of them, for I am with you."

JEREMIAH 1:6–8

December 5

"*I*T IS NOT BY strength that one prevails."... Reaching into his bag and taking out a stone, [David] slung it and struck the Philistine on the forehead.... He fell facedown on the ground. So David triumphed over the Philistine with a sling and a stone.—I delight in weaknesses.... For when I am weak, then I am strong.

1 SAMUEL 2:9; 17:49–50; 2 CORINTHIANS 12:10

December 6

*H*E CHOSE TO GIVE us birth through the word of truth, that we might be a kind of firstfruits of all he created.—
We are God's workmanship, created in Christ Jesus to do good works, which God prepared in advance for us to do.

JAMES 1:18; EPHESIANS 2:10

December 7

*T*HE MEEKNESS AND GENTLENESS of Christ.—A bruised reed he will not break, and a smoldering wick he will not snuff out.... He tends his flock like a shepherd: He gathers the lambs in his arms and carries them close to his heart; he gently leads those that have young.

2 CORINTHIANS 10:1; ISAIAH 42:3; 40:11

December 8

BROTHERS, IF SOMEONE IS caught in a sin, you who are spiritual should restore him gently.—If one of you should wander from the truth and someone should bring him back, remember this: Whoever turns a sinner from the error of his way will save him from death and cover over a multitude of sins.

GALATIANS 6:1; JAMES 5:19–20

December 9

TO DO WHAT IS right and just is more acceptable to the Lord than sacrifice.—"To love him with all your heart, with all your understanding and with all your strength, and to love your neighbor as yourself is more important than all burnt offerings and sacrifices."

PROVERBS 21:3; MARK 12:33

December 10

"*T*HEN YOU WILL KNOW the truth, and the truth will set you free." They answered him, "We are Abraham's descendants and have never been slaves of anyone. How can you say that we shall be set free?" Jesus replied, "I tell you the truth, everyone who sins is a slave to sin.... So if the Son sets you free, you will be free indeed."

JOHN 8:32–34, 36

December 11

"*W*AKE UP, O SLEEPER, rise from the dead, and Christ will shine on you."— "Arise, shine, for your light has come, and the glory of the Lord rises upon you. See, darkness covers the earth and thick darkness is over the peoples, but the Lord rises upon you and his glory appears over you."

EPHESIANS 5:14; ISAIAH 60:1–2

December 12

STRENGTHEN THE FEEBLE HANDS, steady the knees that give way; say to those with fearful hearts, "Be strong, do not fear; your God will come, he will come with vengeance; with divine retribution he will come to save you."—"The LORD your God is with you, he is mighty to save. He will take great delight in you."

ISAIAH 35:3–4; ZEPHANIAH 3:17

December 13

BE STRONG IN THE grace that is in Christ Jesus.—Being strengthened with all power according to his glorious might—Just as you received Christ Jesus as Lord, continue to live in him, rooted and built up in him—They will be called oaks of right-eousness, a planting of the Lord for the display of his splendor.

2 TIMOTHY 2:1; COLOSSIANS 1:11; 2:6–7; ISAIAH 61:3

December 14

SING THE GLORY OF his name; make his praise glorious! —I will praise God's name in song and glorify him with thanksgiving.—[They] sang the song of Moses the servant of God and the song of the Lamb: "Great and marvelous are your deeds, Lord God Almighty."

PSALM 66:2; 69:30; REVELATION 15:3

December 15

CARRY EACH OTHER'S BURDENS.—LOOK not only to your own interests, but also to the interests of others.—Rejoice with those who rejoice; mourn with those who mourn.—Live in harmony with one another; be sympathetic, love as brothers, be compassionate and humble.

GALATIANS 6:2; PHILIPPIANS 2:4; ROMANS 12:15;
1 PETER 3:8

December 16

GOD HAS REVEALED IT to us by his Spirit.—"The knowledge of the secrets of the kingdom of heaven has been given to you."—We have not received the spirit of the world but the Spirit who is from God, that we may understand what God has freely given us.

1 CORINTHIANS 2:10; MATTHEW 13:11;

1 CORINTHIANS 2:12

December 17

THE SPIRIT GIVES LIFE.—THE Spirit helps us in our weakness. . . . The Spirit intercedes for the saints in accordance with God's will.—"The words I have spoken to you are spirit and they are life."—And no one can say, "Jesus is Lord," except by the Holy Spirit.

JOHN 6:63; ROMANS 8:26–27; JOHN 6:63;

1 CORINTHIANS 12:3

December 18

WHERE THE SPIRIT OF the Lord is, there is freedom.—Through Christ Jesus the law of the Spirit of life set me free from the law of sin and death.—It is for freedom that Christ has set us free. Stand firm, then, and do not let yourselves be burdened again by a yoke of slavery.

2 CORINTHIANS 3:17; ROMANS 8:2; GALATIANS 5:1

December 19

"I HAVE COMPASSION FOR these people; they have already been with me three days and have nothing to eat. I do not want to send them away hungry, or they may collapse on the way."—People were bringing little children to Jesus to have him touch them.... And he took the children in his arms, put his hands on them and blessed them.

MATTHEW 15:32; MARK 10:13, 16

December 20

"*L*OOK, EVEN IF THE LORD should open the floodgates of the heavens, could this happen?"—"Have faith in God."—"Test me in this," says the LORD Almighty, "and see if I will not throw open the flood-gates of heaven and pour out so much blessing that you will not have room enough for it."

2 KINGS 7:2; MARK 11:22; MALACHI 3:10

December 21

*G*OD HEARD THE BOY crying, and the angel of God called to Hagar from heaven and said to her, "What is the matter, Hagar? Do not be afraid; God has heard the boy crying as he lies there." ... Then God opened her eyes and she saw a well of water. So she went and filled the skin with water and gave the boy a drink.

GENESIS 21:17, 19

December 22

"WHERE IS THIS 'COMING' he promised?"—"See, the Lord is coming with thousands upon thousands of his holy ones to judge everyone, and to convict all the ungodly of all the ungodly acts they have done."—Look, he is coming with the clouds, and every eye will see him, even those who pierced him.

2 PETER 3:4; JUDE 14–15; REVELATION 1:7

December 23

GOD PRESENTED HIM AS a sacrifice of atonement, through faith in his blood. He did this to demonstrate his justice, because in his forbearance he had left the sins committed beforehand unpunished—he did it to demonstrate his justice at the present time, so as to be just and the one who justifies the man who has faith in Jesus.

ROMANS 3:25–26

December 24

*I*F YOU LIVE ACCORDING to the sinful nature, you will die; but if by the Spirit you put to death the misdeeds of the body, you will live.—Those who belong to Christ Jesus have crucified the sinful nature with its passions and desires. Since we live by the Spirit, let us keep in step with the Spirit.

ROMANS 8:13; GALATIANS 5:24–25

December 25

*T*HANKS BE TO GOD for his indescribable gift!—For to us a child is born, to us a son is given, and the government will be on his shoulders. And he will be called Wonderful Counselor, Mighty God, Everlasting Father, Prince of Peace.—"He had one left to send, a son, whom he loved."

2 CORINTHIANS 9:15; ISAIAH 9:6; MARK 12:6

December 26

"*H*E WHO STANDS FIRM to the end will be saved."—"The seed on good soil stands for those with a noble and good heart, who hear the word, retain it, and by persevering produce a crop."—By faith you stand firm.

MATTHEW 24:13; LUKE 8:15; 2 CORINTHIANS 1:24

December 27

*G*OD WAS RECONCILING THE world to himself in Christ, not counting men's sins against them.—Once you were alienated from God and were enemies in your minds because of your evil behavior. But now he has reconciled you by Christ's physical body through death to present you holy in his sight, without blemish and free from accusation.

2 CORINTHIANS 5:19; COLOSSIANS 1:21–22

December 28

"SON, YOUR SINS ARE forgiven."—
"I will forgive their wickedness and will
remember their sins no more."—"Who can
forgive sins but God alone?"—"I, even I,
am he who blots out your transgressions,
for my own sake, and remembers your sins
no more."—In Christ God forgave you.

MARK 2:5; JEREMIAH 31:34; MARK 2:7; ISAIAH 43:25;
EPHESIANS 4:32

December 29

COME NEAR TO GOD and he will come
near to you.—Do two walk together unless
they have agreed to do so?—The Lord is
with you when you are with him. If you
seek him, he will be found by you.—"You
will seek me and find me when you seek me
with all your heart."

JAMES 4:8; AMOS 3:3; 2 CHRONICLES 15:2;
JEREMIAH 29:13

December 30

I GUIDE YOU IN the way of wisdom and lead you along straight paths. When you walk, your steps will not be hampered; when you run, you will not stumble.... Do not set foot on the path of the wicked or walk in the way of evil men. Avoid it, do not travel on it; turn from it and go on your way.

PROVERBS 4:11–12, 14–15

December 31

"*T*HE LORD YOUR GOD carried you, as a father carries his son, all the way you went until you reached this place."—In his love and mercy he redeemed them; he lifted them up and carried them.—"Even to your old age and gray hairs I am he, I am he who will sustain you. I have made you and I will carry you."

DEUTERONOMY 1:31; ISAIAH 63:9; 46:4

The Sermon on the Mount

Blessed are the poor in spirit,
   for theirs is the kingdom of heaven.
Blessed are those who mourn,
   for they will be comforted.
Blessed are the meek,
   for they will inherit the earth.
Blessed are those who hunger and thirst for
righteousness,
   for they will be filled.
 Blessed are the merciful,
   for they will be shown mercy.
Blessed are the pure in heart,
   for they will see God.
Blessed are the peacemakers,
   for they will be called sons of God.
Blessed are those who are persecuted
because of righteousness,
   for theirs is the kingdom of heaven.

Matthew 5:3-10

The Lord's Prayer

Our Father which art in heaven,
   Hallowed be thy name.
Thy kingdom come.
Thy will be done in earth,
   as it is in heaven.
Give us this day our daily bread.
And forgive us our debts,
   as we forgive our debtors. And lead us
   not into temptation, but deliver us from
evil:
For thine is the kingdom, and the power,
   and the glory, for ever. Amen.

Matthew 6:9-13 KJV

189